TABLE OF CONTENTS

★ Administration Information

★ Student Resources & FAQ

★ Semester Calendar

★ Studio Class Schedule

★ Student Store

★ Lesson Success

★ Recital Information

★ "What Songs am I Playing On?" Checklist

★ Earn Your Wings

★ Sheet Music

★ Practice Activities & Coloring Sheets

MEET THE ADMIN TEAM

Teamwork makes the dream work!

At Snake River Strings Company, we are increasing our efforts to speed up our response time & help you with your questions as fast as we can. That's why we created our administration team! The team's purpose is to make your life- & Shelby's!- easier. Feel free to reach out to us whenever you need!

Mon. - Fri. 10:00 am - 8:00 pm | 208-681-0035 | snakeriverstringsco@gmail.com

Lizzy Wada

Lizzy started fiddling with SRSC back when we were still Snake River Fiddle Club! She is very grateful for the opportunity to work with Shelby again, and to see all of the students' progress. Lizzy is a current student of BYU Provo, & loves board games, theatre, cheese, & listening almost exclusively to The Collection, Oshima Brothers, & Wild Rivers.

- New student sign up
- Scheduling conflicts
- Opus support
- Withdrawals
- Billing
- Grant programs

Madyson Clark

- Pocatello Receptionist
- Trial lesson follow-up
- Scheduling conflicts
- Opus support
- Tiktok Content Creator

We are so excited to have Madyson doubling as an instructor and receptionist here at SRSC! Maddy loves spending time outdoors, writing songs, & working out. She loves music "because it has always gotten me through hard times and has always been a safe place for me." Madyson thinks that SRSC has the best students, staff, and teachers ever!

Remember!

We are humans too! We want to make life and lessons as easy as we can for you, and we are not immune to mistakes and misunderstandings. Please remember to be kind in your communications, and we will help you as best as we can.
Thank you!

STUDENT RESOURCES

We have so many resources available to help you in your music journey, and they are all readily available on our website **snakeriverstringsco.com** !

Site Header

About Lessons Students Locations

① Student Login
② Calendar
③ Recital Sign-up
④ Studio Updates
⑤ Policies

① Login to Opus Student Portal + Opus tutorial videos!

② View monthly student calendar

③ Sign up for semester recitals & access recital information

④ Get the latest on studio updates & student of the month

⑤ Become familiar with studio policies

Opus FAQ

The "Student Login" tab has the link to access Opus, as well as tutorial videos for logging in, cancelling lessons & scheduling makeup credits, and accessing lesson notes & communicating with your teacher.

If these videos don't answer your questions, feel free to give us a call or send a text! If possible, please send us screenshots of issues so we can know more of how to help you.

OPUS STUDENT PORTAL TUTORIALS

Logging into Opus

Cancelling Lessons and Booking Makeup Credits on Opus

September 2023

SUN	MON	TUES	WED	THURS	FRI	SAT
					1 No lessons- back to school	**2**
3	**4** No Lessons- Labor Day	**5**	**6**	**7**	**8**	**9**
10	**11** Lesson 2	**12** Lesson 1	**13** Lesson 1	**14** Lesson 1	**15** Lesson 1	**16**
17	**18** Lesson 3	**19** Lesson 2	**20** Lesson 2	**21** Lesson 2	**22** Lesson 2	**23**
24	**25** Blackfoot General Studio Class Beginner 4:30-5:15 Int. 5:30-6:15 Adv/Adult	**26** Pocatello Studio Class Beginner 4:30-5:15 Int. 5:30-6:15 Adv/Adult 6:30-7:15	**27** Blackfoot Rock Studio Class Beginner 4:30-5:15 Int. 5:30-6:15	**28** Pocatello Studio Class Songwriting 5:30-6:15	**29** Lesson 3	**30** Autumnal Equinox

NOTES: **See here for more updates on Studio Class schedules and registration!**

*Subject to change. Make sure to always refer to opus for most up to date information.

October 2023

SUN	MON	TUES	WED	THURS	FRI	SAT
1	2	3	4	5	6	7
8	9 Lesson 1	10 Lesson 1	11 Lesson 1	12 Lesson 1	13 Lesson 1	14
15	16 Lesson 2	17 Lesson 2	18 Lesson 2	19 Lesson 2	20 Lesson 2	21
22	23 Lesson 3 Blackfoot General Studio Class Beginner 4:30-5:15 Int. 5:30-6:15 Adv/Adult 6:	24 Lesson 3 Pocatello Studio Class Beginner 4:30-5:15 Int. 5:30-6:15 Avd/Adult 6:30-7:15	25 Lesson 3 Blackfoot Rock Studio Class Beginner 4:30-5:15 Int. 5:30-6:15 Adv/Adult 6:30-7:15	26 Lesson 3 Pocatello Studio Class Songwriting 5:30-6:15	27 Lesson 3	28
29	30 Lesson 1	31 Last day to RSVP for the recital! Lesson 1				

NOTES

See here for more updates on Studio Class schedules and registration!

*Subject to change. Make sure to always refer to opus for most up to date information.

November 2023

SUN	MON	TUES	WED	THURS	FRI	SAT
			1	2	3	4
5 Daylight Saving Time Ends	6	7	8 Lesson 1	9 Lesson 1	10 Lesson 1	11 Rehearsal for Recital / Veterans Day
12	13 Lesson 2	14 Lesson 2	15 Lesson 2	16 Lesson 2	17 Lesson 2	18 Fall Rehearsal & Recital
19	20 Lesson 3	21 Lesson 3	22 Lesson 3	23 No lessons Thanksgiving Day	24 No lessons	25
26	27 No lessons	28 Lesson 1	29 Lesson 1	30 Lesson 1		

NOTES See here for more updates on Studio Class schedules and registration!

*Subject to change. Make sure to always refer to opus for most up to date information.

December 2023

SUN	MON	TUES	WED	THURS	FRI	SAT
					1	2
3	4	5	6	7	8 Lesson 1	9
10	11 Lesson 2	12 Lesson 2	13 Lesson 2	14 Lesson 2	15 Lesson 2	16
17	18 Lesson 3	19 Lesson 3	20 Lesson 3	21 Lesson 3	22 Lesson 3	23
	Blackfoot General Studio Class Beginner 4:30-5:15 Int. 5:30-6:15 Adv/Adult 6:	Pocatello Studio Class Beginner 4:30-5:15 Int. 5:30-6:15 Adv/Adult 6:30-7:15	Blackfoot Rock Studio Class Beginner 4:30-5:15 Int. 5:30-6:15 Adv/Adult 6:30-7:15	Pocatello Studio Class Songwriting 5:30-6:15		
24 Christmas Eve	25 no lessons Christmas Day	26 no lessons	27 no lessons	28 no lessons	29 no lessons	30
31 New Year's Eve						

NOTES

See here for more updates on Studio Class schedules and registration!

*Subject to change. Make sure to always refer to opus for most up to date information.

STUDIO SESSIONS
SEPT, OCT, & DEC 2023

Our goal with studio classes is to provide an opportunity for students who take private lessons to build community among the other students, to give an application for what you're working on in private lessons, to learn from our other incredible instructors, and to learn how to apply yourself in a group setting. Instead of private lessons, we offer these elective classes on the 4th week of each month. As a student of SRSC you are welcome to attend as many as you'd like for free! Please register for the classes you'd like to attend below.

DAY & TIME	MONDAY	TUESDAY	WEDNESDAY	THURSDAY
4:30-5:15	**BLACKFOOT BEGINNER STUDIO CLASS** Open to all instruments. This class is more geared towards those under 11 years old. Students will get to know each other, perform a song for the group, and play through the beginner recital songs: Top Gun, My Country Tis of Thee & Yankee Doodle	**POCATELLO BEGINNER STUDIO CLASS** Open to all instruments. This class is more geared towards those under 11 years old. Students will get to know each other, perform a song for the group, and play through the beginner recital songs: Top Gun, My Country Tis of Thee & Yankee Doodle	**BLACKFOOT BEGINNER ROCK STUDIO CLASS** Open to all instruments. This class is more geared towards those under 11 years old. Students will get to know each other and will play through the beginner recital songs: Top Gun, My Country Tis of Thee & Yankee Doodle	
5:30-6:15	**BLACKFOOT INTERMEDIATE STUDIO CLASS** Open to all instruments. This class is more geared towards those ages 12-14. Students will get to know each other, perform a song for the group, and play through the intermediate recital songs: Top Gun, America The Beautiful, Ashokan Farewell, Soldier's Joy, & This Land is Your Land	**POCATELLO INTERMEDIATE STUDIO CLASS** Open to all instruments. This class is more geared towards those ages 12-14. Students will get to know each other, perform a song for the group, and play through the intermediate recital songs: Top Gun, America The Beautiful, Ashokan Farewell, Soldier's Joy, & This Land is Your Land	**BLACKFOOT INTERMEDIATE ROCK STUDIO CLASS** Open to all instruments. This class is more geared towards those 12-14 years old. Students will get to know each other and will play through the intermediate recital songs: Top Gun, America The Beautiful, Ashokan Farewell, Soldier's Joy, & This Land is Your Land	**POCATELLO SONGWRITING CLASS** Come learn how to write and workshop a song! Open to all instruments and ages.
6:30-7:15	**BLACKFOOT ADVANCED AND ADULT STUDIO CLASS** Open to all instruments. This class is more geared towards high school to adult. Students will get to know each other, perform a song for the group, and play through the advanced recital songs: Top Gun Anthem, Star Spangled Banner, and Army Branches Song.	**POCATELLO ADVANCED AND ADULT STUDIO CLASS** Open to all instruments. This class is more geared towards high school to adult. Students will get to know each other, perform a song for the group, and play through the advanced recital songs: Top Gun Anthem, Star Spangled Banner, Born in the USA, and Army Branches Song.	**BLACKFOOT ADVANCED AND ADULT ROCK STUDIO CLASS** Open to all instruments. This class is more geared towards high school to adult. Students will get to know each other and will play through the advanced recital songs: Top Gun Anthem, Star Spangled Banner, Born in the USA, and Army Branches Song.	

Scan here to register for a class

FALL RECITAL
NOVEMBER 18, 2023 @ 2PM

https://snakeriverstringsco.opus1.io/w/summerstudiosessions

STUDENT STORE

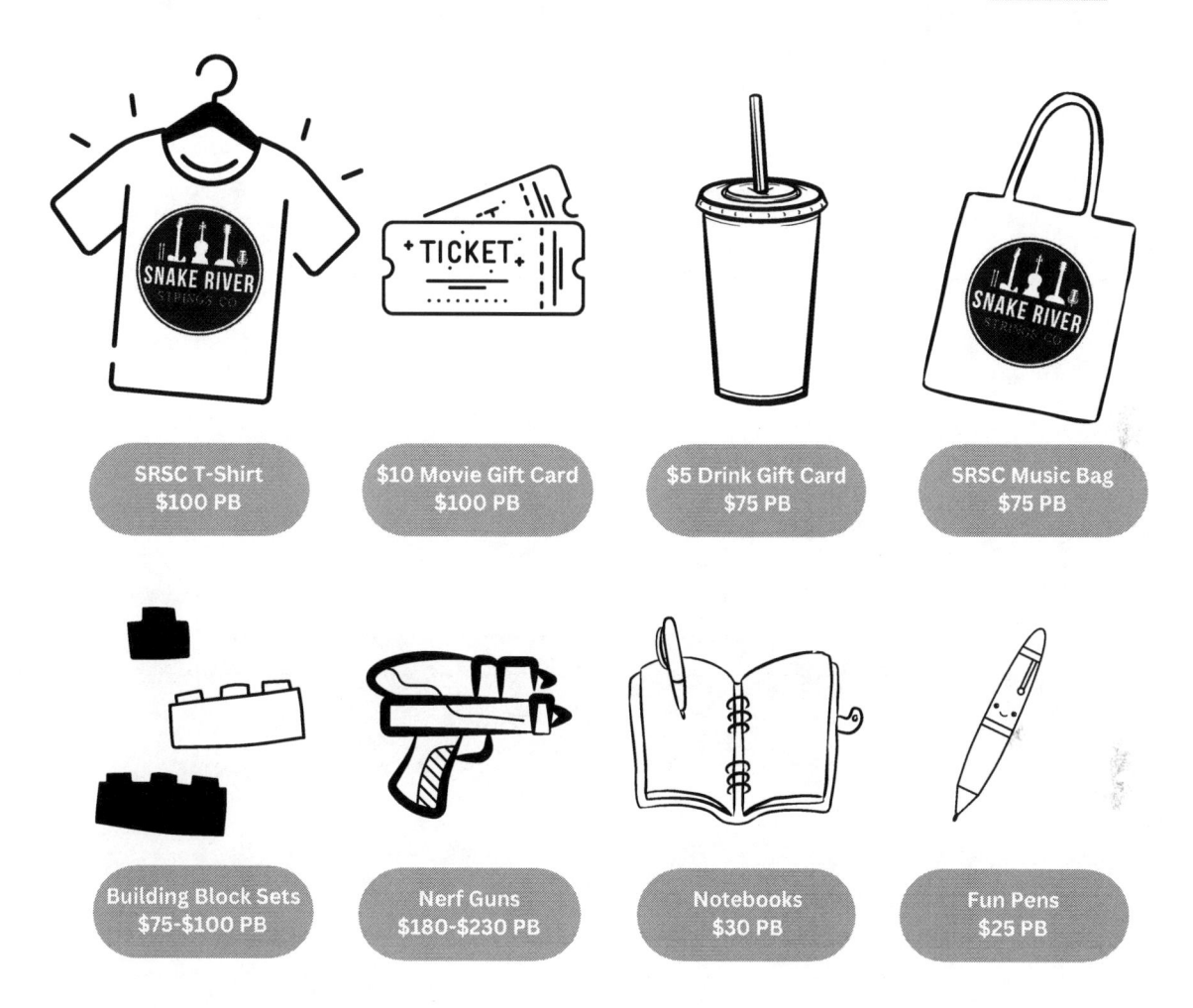

SRSC T-Shirt
$100 PB

$10 Movie Gift Card
$100 PB

$5 Drink Gift Card
$75 PB

SRSC Music Bag
$75 PB

Building Block Sets
$75-$100 PB

Nerf Guns
$180-$230 PB

Notebooks
$30 PB

Fun Pens
$25 PB

WHAT ARE PB?

PB stands for "Practice Bucks!" That means- you guessed it- you get money for practicing! PB are given out at weekly lessons by your student's instructor. We know that learning new things can be tough & challenging, so we believe in rewarding our kids when they go out of their comfort zones!

Ways to earn PB include **coming to lessons, practicing, participating in studio class, performing at a concert, writing a review on Google, & tagging us on social media!**

We are always on the lookout for new things to add to our store, so keep an eye out for new additions every week!

GUIDE TO LESSON SUCCESS

- Encourage your student to P R A C T I C E
- Push your student to try new things
- Attend occasional lessons with your student
- Inform teacher of student's needs/your expectations
- Attend concerts & support live local music!
- Become familiar with studio policy
- Invite family to your students' events & CHEER THEM ON

PRACTICE TOOLBOX

Playing with cello drones (found on YouTube) improves intonation!

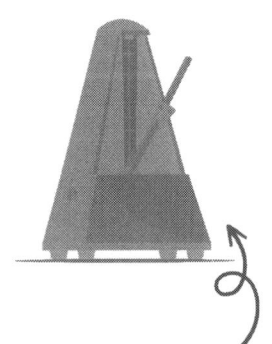

A metronome will help you keep the beat & develop rhythm!

Listening to lesson recordings lets you mimic your teacher & learn from their style!

SNAKE RIVER STRINGS CO

Snake River Strings Co. Fall 2023 Recital

LET FREEDOM RING WITH SNAKE RIVER STRINGS

Saturday November 18, 2023
Blackfoot Performing Arts Center
2:00 PM

We are super excited for our 5th annual themed recital! This year's theme is "Let Freedom Ring with Snake River Strings" and will feature big group numbers, small group numbers, instructor performances, and student solos. We will be performing patriotic songs, and recognizing veterans. We will keep the show's length to one hour.

We will wear SRSC limited edition patriotic t-shirts, we will stay in touch as the recital gets closer with order information. You can accessorize with red, white, and blue items or aviator glasses.

Your teacher will help you fill out the following page, which will tell you what songs you need to prepare for the recital, and what rehearsals you need to attend. It is expected that you work on these pieces in addition to your personal repertoire this semester. Our goal is to create well-rounded musicians that can perform a wide array of music, as well as have fun creating music with others!

- Each performer will get one complimentary ticket to the show, and an RSVP for recital participation is required.
- Recital RSVP will close on October 31, 2022 (Halloween!) so that we can plan accordingly for staging, microphones, and awards.
- Additional tickets for the show can be purchased on our website and at the door.

The sheet music for the recital songs can be found in this booklet. Make sure to read the fun little snippets about each song, and ask your teacher about the "teaching points." Scan the corresponding QR codes to find practice videos and recordings.

Just like playing on a sports team, it is important to do your part in learning the music in order to help the team! It is up to you to practice and make sure you know the materials and attend the rehearsals, if you do so then when we meet together as a group the songs will come together smoothly, and I promise it will be a fun experience for you! Creating music together with others can be very rewarding.

We have worked really hard to arrange these songs for each of you, and are really looking forward to seeing all of the tiny pieces come together to create an amazing showcase! This is going to be a fun semester!

Thank you,
Shelby Murdock
Snake River Strings Co., Owner

LINKS & DATES

Scan this to RSVP for the recital

Make sure to register for text reminders for studio class rehearsals

Submit names of family members that are veterans to be recognized at the concert

Scan this to PURCHASE TICKETS

Dates to remember...
- September 25-28 studio class rehearsal
- October 23-26 studio class rehearsal
- October 31, recital rsvp due!
- November 11 dress rehearsal time TBD
- November 18 mandatory dress rehearsal 10-12am, call time is 1:30, show starts at 2

WHAT SONGS AM I PLAYING ON?

- Check which of the following songs the above student will be performing at the recital (and indicate which part when applicable)

Beginner
- [ ] My Country Tis of Thee
- [ ] Yankee Doodle

Intermediate
- [ ] America The Beautiful
- [ ] Ashokan Farewell
- [ ] Soldier's Joy
- [ ] This Land is Your Land

Advanced
- [ ] Star Spangled Banner
- [ ] Born in the USA
- [ ] Army Branches Song

Everyone
- [ ] Top Gun Anthem

Cellos
- [ ] Taps

- Should they audition for the solo parts on any of those songs?

- If they will also be performing a solo number please write it here:

- Based off of the above songs you should attend the following rehearsals (check all that apply):
  - [ ] Blackfoot Beginner (Mondays 4:30)
  - [ ] Blackfoot Intermediate (Mondays 5:30)
  - [ ] Blackfoot Advanced (Mondays 6:30)
  - [ ] Pocatello Beginner (Tuesdays 4:30)
  - [ ] Pocatello Intermediate (Tuesdays 5:30)
  - [ ] Pocatello Advanced (Tuesdays 6:30)
  - [ ] Blackfoot Rock Beginner (Wednesdays 4:30)
  - [ ] Blackfoot Rock Intermediate (Wednesdays 5:30)
  - [ ] Blackfoot Rock Advanced (Wednesdays 6:30)

[x] **Saturday November 18, 2023 @ Blackfoot Performing Arts Center**
Mandatory full-dress rehearsal 10AM-12PM

EARN YOUR WINGS

TOP MUSICIAN
SNAKE RIVER STRINGS CO.

Memorize all of the songs you're playing in the concert to earn your wings! Which is a limited edition sticker!!! You'll know if you see another student around with this sticker on their case or water bottle, that they're a top musician that earned their wings!!!

Write down the names of the songs you need to memorize for the concert, and as you memorize them check them off! When completed have your teacher sign at the bottom and turn this paper in to receive your limited edition sticker!

- [ ] _____
- [ ] _____
- [ ] _____
- [ ] _____
- [ ] _____
- [ ] _____

- [ ] _____
- [ ] _____
- [ ] _____
- [ ] _____
- [ ] _____
- [ ] _____

NAME: _____

BRANCH: _____
INSTRUMENT

CAPTAIN SIGN OFF: _____
TEACHER

DATE MISSION COMPLETED: _____

SKITS FOR SONG INTRODUCTIONS

Please read through and let Shelby or Nina know if you are interested in a part!

Commitment for skits include:

- Being at a few rehearsals (more info on that later)
- Memorizing your lines
- Finding your costume
- Helping round up props

SKIT 1: UNCLE SAM

Main Character: a 5-9 year old boy

The main role is to dress up in an Uncle Sam costume and announce (in Uncle Sam WW 1 recruiting poster fashion) the branches of the US Military as the theme songs are being played for veterans in the audience to stand and be recognized.

He will also be in costume the entire show and able to play along in the performances. He will also march over to the performers that have solos and call them out to perform with:

Uncle Sam: "I want you to solo!"

SKIT 2: YANKEE DOODLE INTRO

Cast:
Campers 1 and 2: 3rd grade- 6th grade
Camper 3: K- 6th must be able to solo Yankee Doodle on fiddle, and character acts a little stuck up

Costumes: Plaid Flannel shirt over a T-shirt, jeans

Scene: Around a campfire roasting marshmallows

Camper 1: "I wish I knew some songs we could sing! Campfires are so much more fun with singing!"

Camper 2: "I know a song, but forgot how it goes. It talks about a guy putting a feather in his hat and calling it macaroni and cheese."

Camper 1: "That's Yankee Doodle! But it doesn't have macaroni and cheese in it. It's, "stuck a feather in his hat, and called it macaroni". I learned that when that song was written, macaroni was a term for a man that was well dressed, wealthy, and thought they were big stuff." I can't remember the tune either!!

Camper 1 and 2 roast marshmallows while trying to hum and remember the tune and can't get it. Camper 3 enters.

Camper 3: Grabbing a marshmallow and stick. "Hi! Can I join in?"

Camper 1 and 2: Yep.

Camper 3: "Look out, yours is on fire!" (to Camper 1)

Camper 1: blows out marshmallow. "Hey, do you know the song, 'Yankee Doodle'? (to Camper 3)

Camper 3: "Why sure! EV-ry one knows THAT song! Yours is smokin' and black. (pointing to Camper 2's marshmallow) Hand me that fiddle (Camper 3's instrument hiding behind the campers) and I'll show you how it goes. (pulling their marshmallow out of the fire) Perfectly toasted once again!"

Camper 3 Beings Yankee Doodle while camper 1 and 2 clear stage of props

SKIT 3: ASHOKAN FAREWELL INTRO

Cast: An adult male to read an abbreviated version of Sullivan Ballou's letter to his wife, written one week before his death in the First Battle of Bull Run- July 21, 1861 during the Civil War. SRSCO will play Ashokan Farwell in the background with a possible slideshow (https://youtu.be/1VK1KcZoDu0)

This will be read- doesn't need to be memorized!!

"A week before the battle of Bull Run, Sullivan Ballou, a Major in the 2nd Rhod Island Volunteers, wrote home to his wife in Smithfield.

July 14, 1861
Camp Clark, Washington DC

Dear Sarah:

The indications are very strong that we shall move in a few days- perhaps tomorrow. And lest I should not be able to write you again, I feel impelled to write a few lines that may fall under your eye when I am no more.

I have no misgivings about, or lack of confidence in the cause in which I am engaged, and my courage does not halt or falter. I know how American Civilization now leans upon the triumph of the government and how great a debt we owe to those who went before us through the blood and suffering of the Revolution. And I am willing-perfectly willing-to lay down all my joys in this life, to help maintain this government, and to pay that debt.

Sara, my love for you is deathless, it seems to bind me with mighty cables that nothing but omnipotence can break; and yet my love to Country comes over me like a strong wind and bears me irresistibly with all those chains to the battlefield. The memory of all the blissful moments I have enjoyed with you come crowding over me, and I feel most deeply grateful to God and you, that I have enjoyed them for so long. And how hard it is for me to give them up and burn to ashes the hopes and future years, when, God willing, we might still have lived and loved together, and see our boys grown up to honorable manhood around us.

If I do not return, my dear Sarah, never forget how much I loved you, nor that when my last breath escapes me on the battle field, it will whisper your name…

Forgive my many faults, and the many pains I have caused you. How thoughtless, how foolish I have sometimes been!...

But, O Sarah, if the dead can come back to this earth and flit unseen around those they love, I shall always be with you, in the brightest day and in the darkest night…always, always. And when the soft breeze fans your cheek, it shall be my breath, or the cool air your throbbing temple, it shall be my spirit passing by.

Sarah do not mourn me dead; think I am gone and wait for me, for we shall meet again…

Sullivan Ballou was killed a week later at the 1st Battle of Bull Run"

-from www.jayandmolly.com/ashokan-farewell/the-sullivan-ballou-letter/

SKIT 4: THIS LAND IS MY LAND, THIS LAND IS YOUR LAND INTRO

Cast:
Dad: high school boy
Mom: high school girl
Child 1: anyone
Child 2: anyone

Costume: Probably whatever the overall concert attire is

Scene: Family Vacation in a '80s VW van (Walking on stage from audience)

Child 1: (whining) "He (or she depending on cast) pinched me!"
Child 2: "Did not! She hit me first!"
Mom: "Stop it! Why don't y'all sing a song to pass time?"
Child 1 and 2: "99 bottles of pop on the wall, 99 bottles of pop!"
Dad and Mom: frustrated sounds

On stage, but still in van

Child 2: "Why didn't we take a plane for this trip? It would have been SOOO much faster!"
Child 1: "Yah, I've never been on a plane."
Dad: Because we want to SEE the sights, FEEL the road beneath our feet, and have the air blowing in our face! Aww!
Mom: "AC would be nice right about now… but I do agree that a road trip was the way to do this trip! Think about it, we've made it all the way from the redwood forest to Devil's Tower, to Mt. Rushmore, to St. Louis Arch, to George Washington's home at Mt. Vernon, to now- almost the Statue of Liberty! This land surely was 'made for you and me'!"

Walks/drives off stage and song starts.

TOP GUN ANTHEM

"Top Gun Anthem" is an instrumental rock composition and the theme of the Top Gun media franchise, including the original 1986 film Top Gun and its 2022 sequel Maverick. Harold Faltermeyer wrote the music with Steve Stevens playing guitar and Flatermeyer on the keyboard in the original recording. Word has it that Stevens recorded the entire part on one track with no overdubs.

Faltermeyer said the he had "no briefing" ahead of composing Top Gun Anthem, other than being told to imagine that the pilots "are like rock n' rollers in the sky." "It was a rare situation where I composed the theme before the movie was shot," he confirmed.

You'll notice this piece has some tricky key changes, you can choose to think enharmonically if you would like!

We will be performing this at the very beginning of the program, with the lights down, while walking up to the stage. So memorization is important!

Make sure to listen to the practice recordings below A LOT! That will help you hear the key changes, and know when your part is supposed to come in.

Ask your Teacher

1. What does enharmonic mean?
2. What are the two enharmonic keys you could think of?
3. What two written key signatures does the song switch between?

SCAN HERE FOR PRACTICE RECORDINGS

PRACTICE NOTES

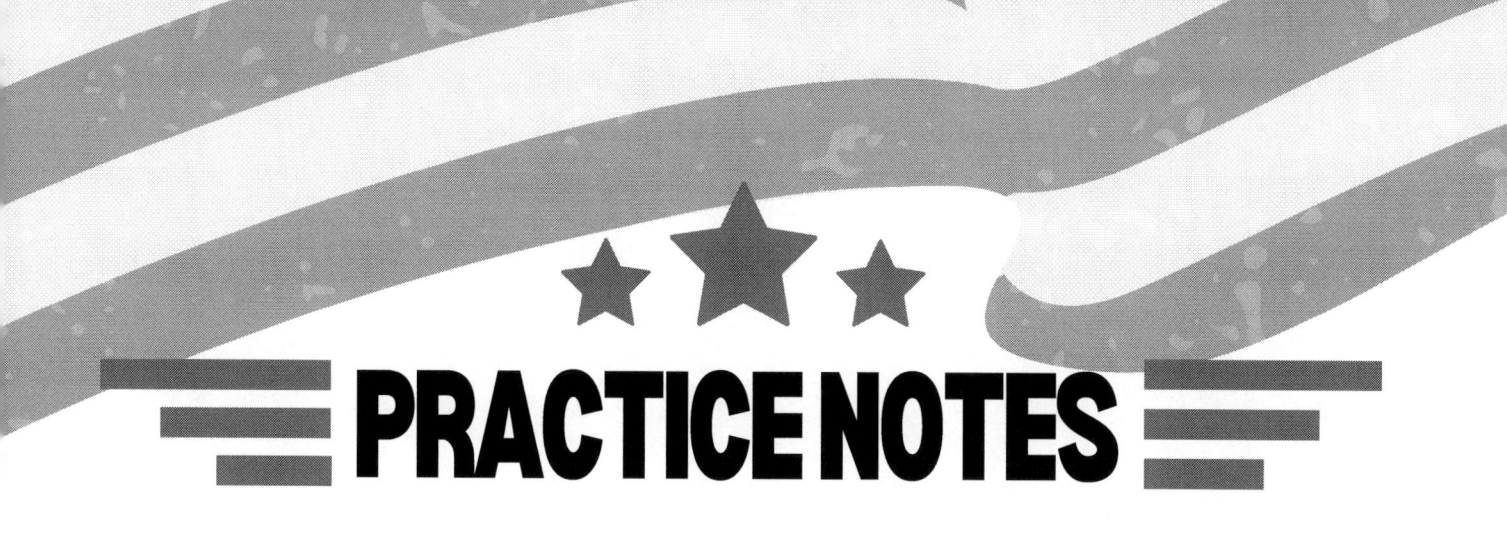

Guitar 1

Top Gun Anthem

Faltermeyer & Stevens
S. Murdock

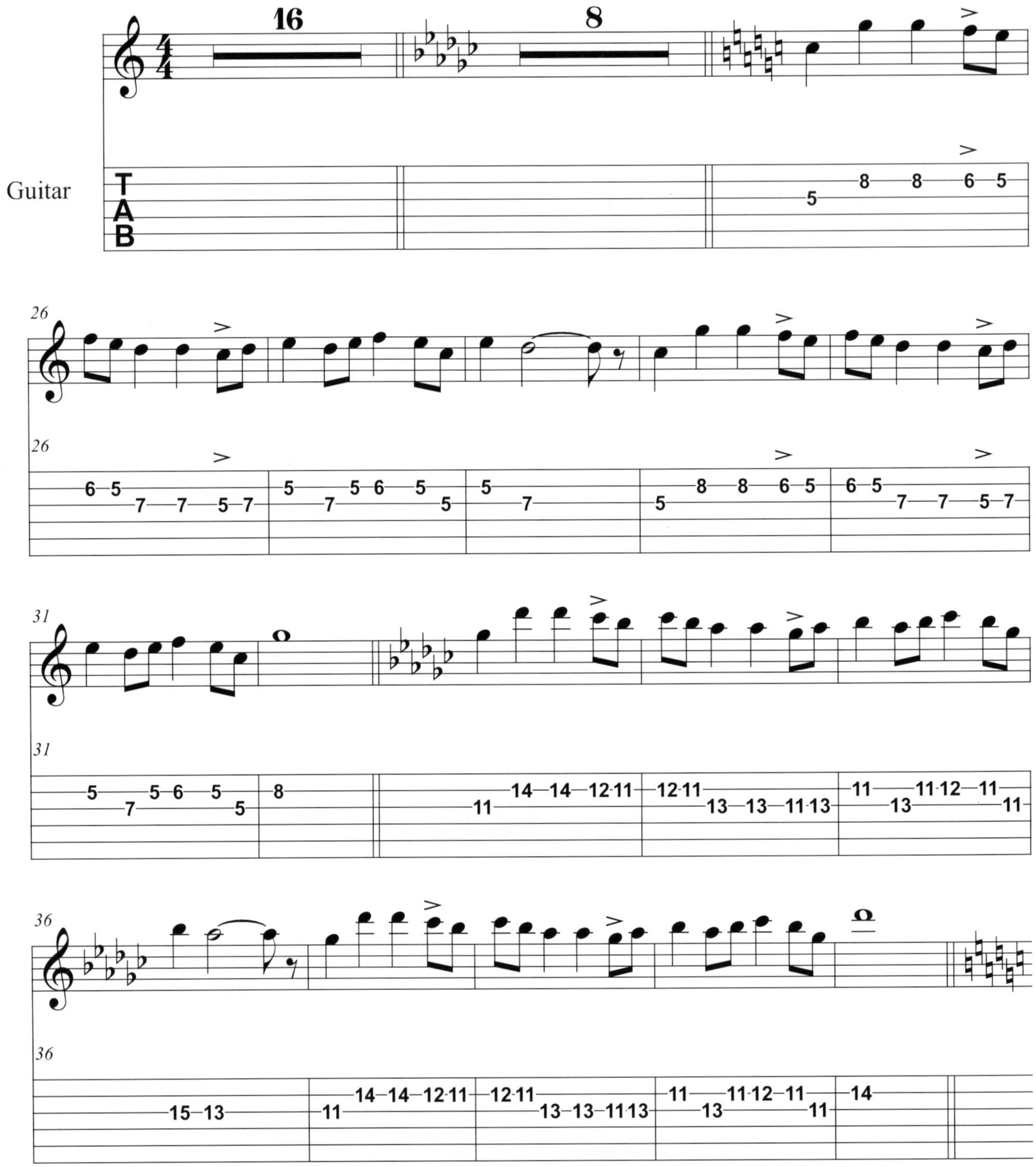

Top Gun Anthem

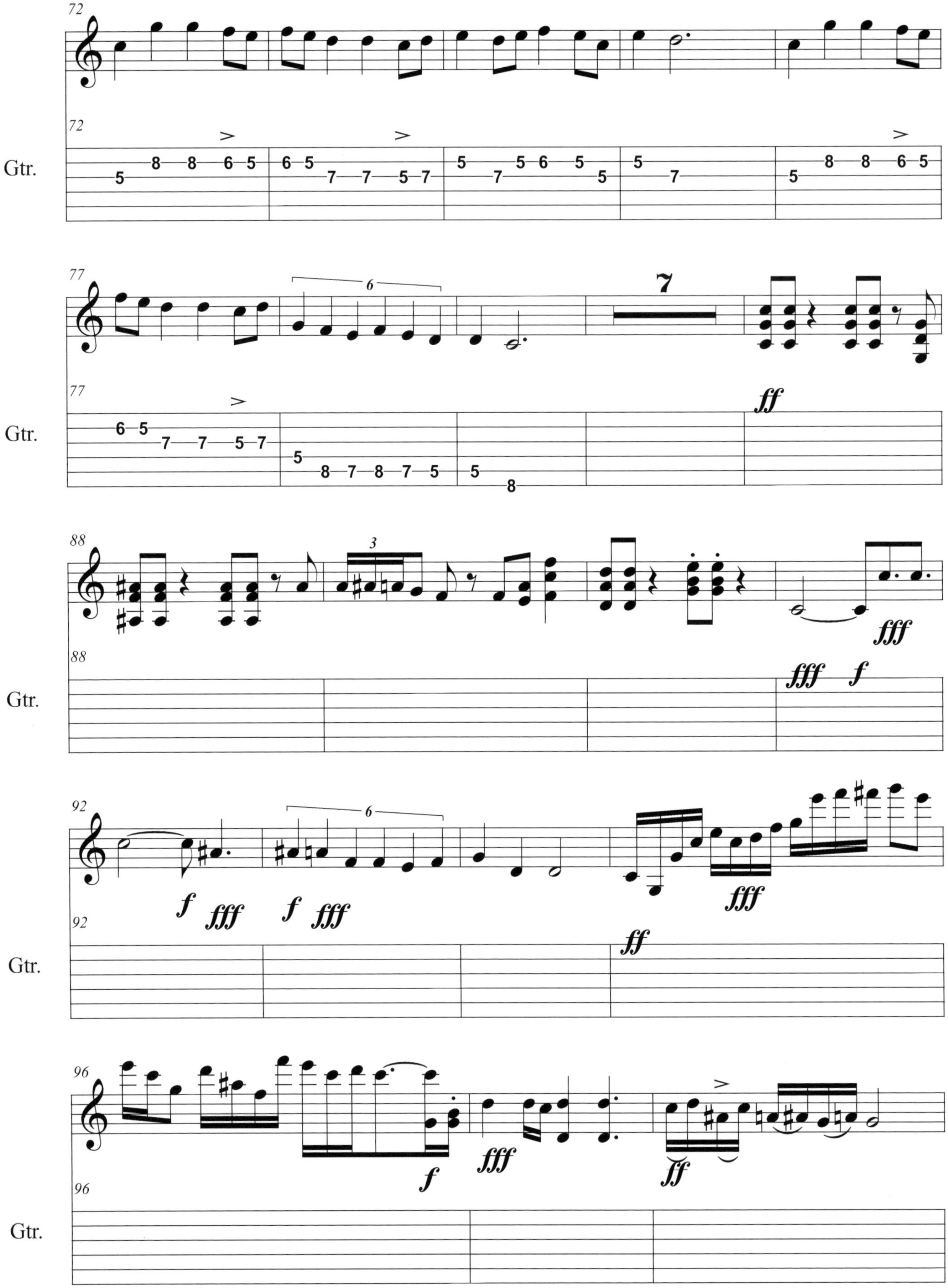
72
Gtr.
77
Gtr.
88
Gtr.
92
Gtr.
96
Gtr.

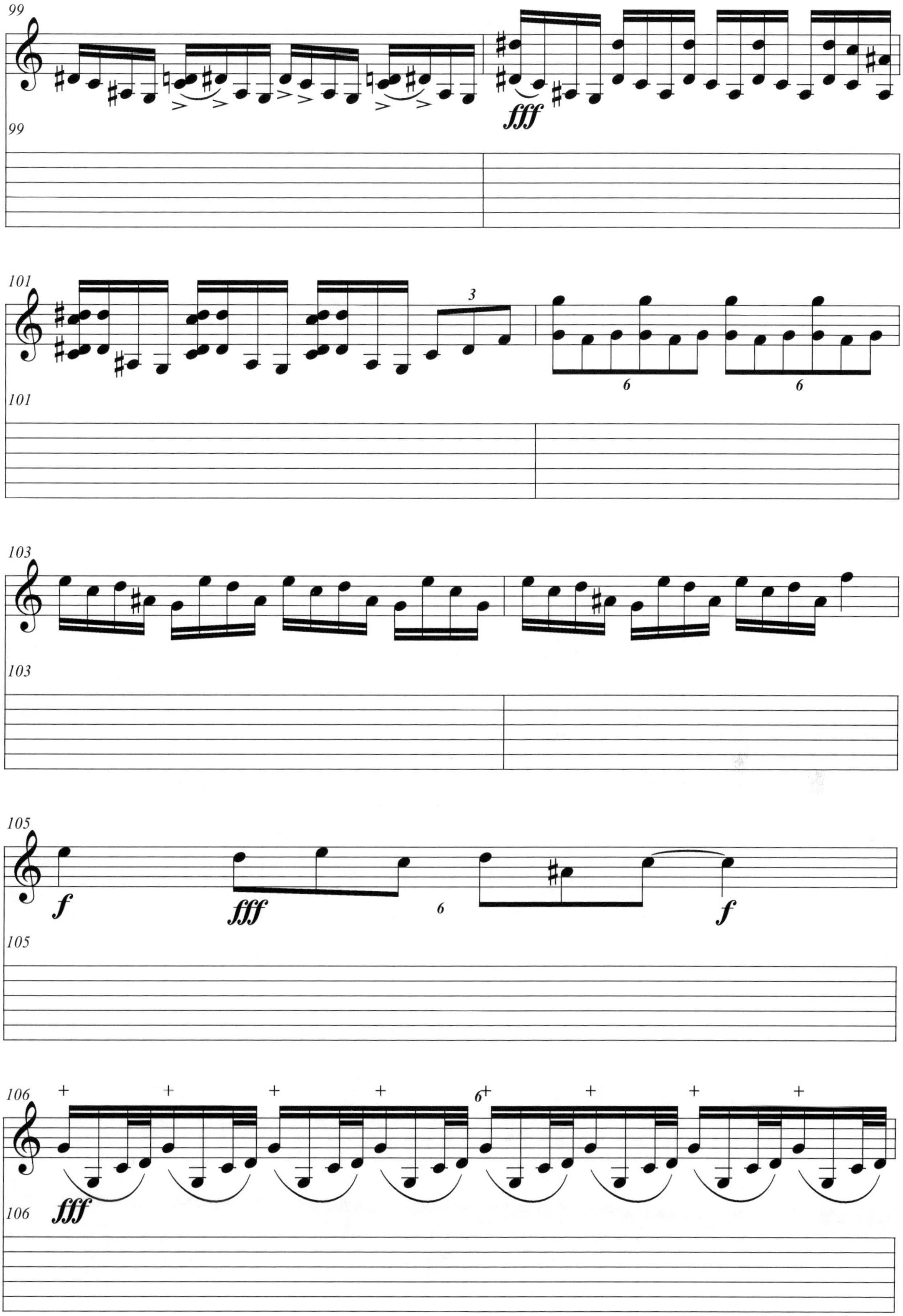
Gtr.
Gtr.
Gtr.
Gtr.
Gtr.

Top Gun Anthem

Top Gun Anthem

Guitar 2

Top Gun Anthem

Faltermeyer & Stevens
S. Murdock

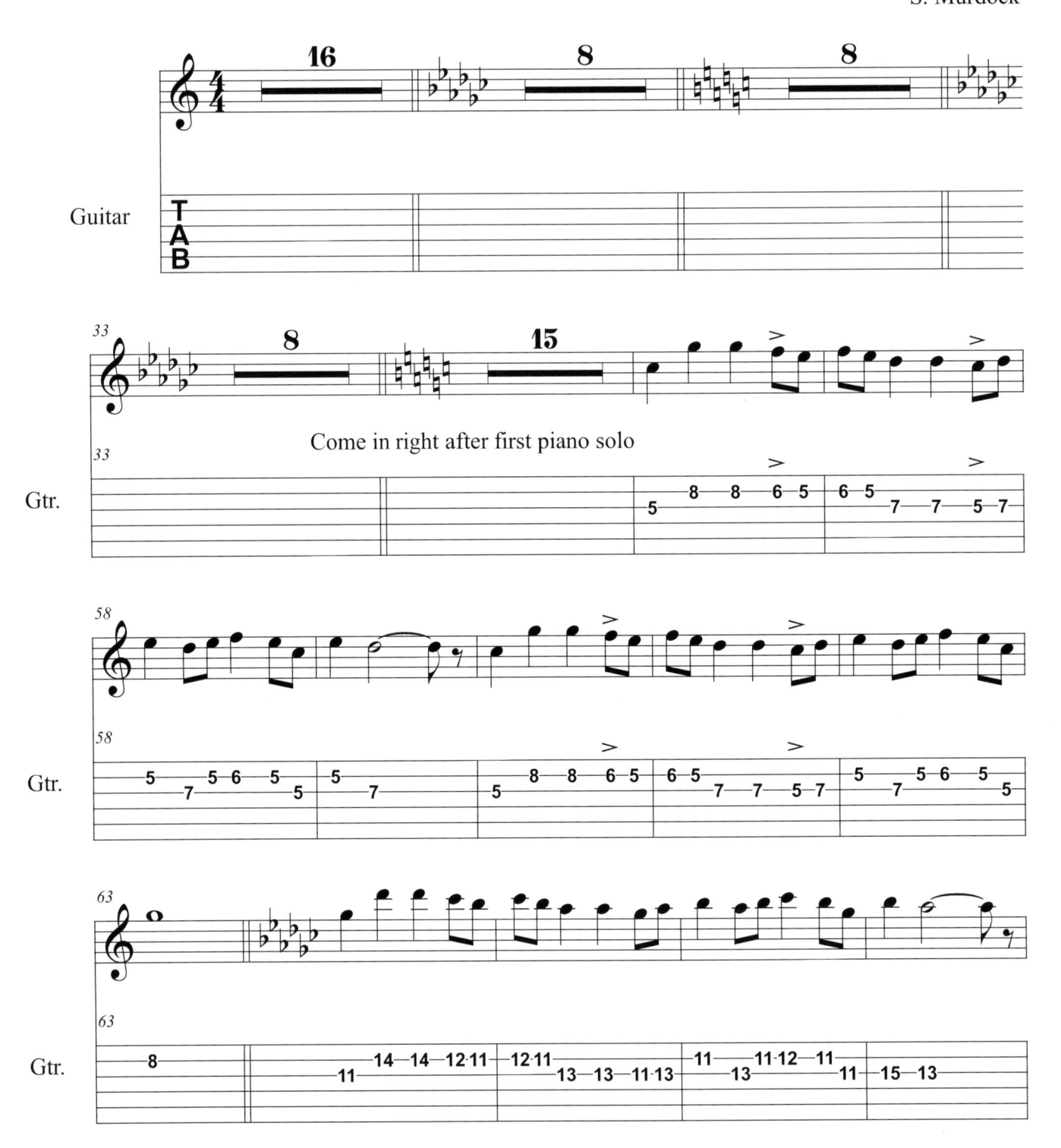

Come in right after first piano solo

©Snake River Strings Co. 2023

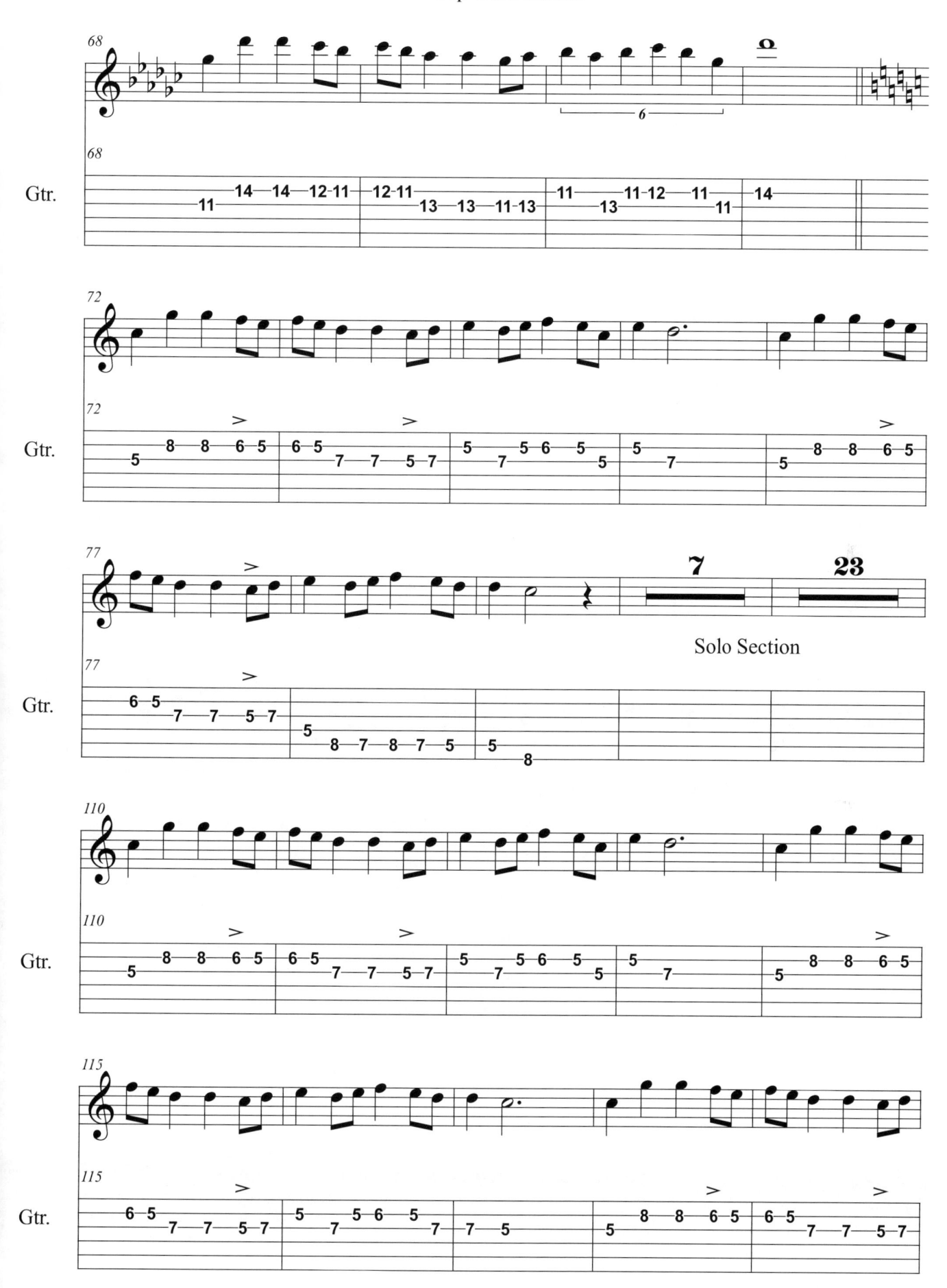

Top Gun Anthem

Solo section chords:

Top Gun Anthem - part I
guitar

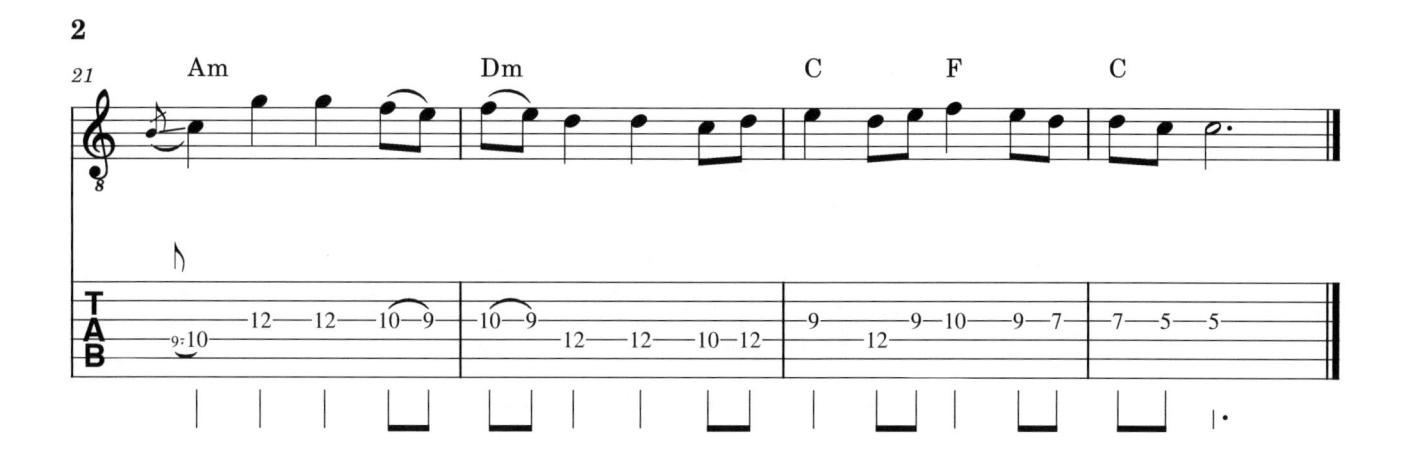

MY COUNTRYTIS OF THEE

When Samuel Francis Smith penned the lines to our "unofficial national anthem" in 1832, he wanted to create a hymn of thanksgiving for our wonderful land. Using a scrap of paper, he scratched out his poem of gratitude in less than 30 minutes. It was first performed by a Children's Choir on July 8, 1831.

The chosen tune was a widely known, and already patriotic tune, "God Save the King"- England's national anthem to set his lyrics to. The tune has no documented original composer or birthplace, but famous composers such as, but not limited to: Bach, Beethoven, Clementi, Debussy, Haydn, Liszt, Paganini, and Strauss have all composed classical orchestra pieces with this tune as the theme of their piece.

<u>My Country 'Tis OF Thee</u>
My country, 'tis of thee,
Sweet land of liberty,
of thee I sing:
Land where my fathers died,
Land of the pilgrims' pride'
From every mountainside
Let freedom ring!

My native country, thee,
Land of the noble free,
Thy name I love;
I love thy rocks and rills,
Thy woods and templed hills;
My heart with rapture thrills
Like that above.

Let music swell the breeze,
And ring from all the trees
Sweet freedom's song:
Let mortal tongues awake,
Let all that breath partake;
Let rocks their silence break,
The sound prolong.

SCAN HERE FOR PRACTICE RECORDINGS

PRACTICE NOTES

My Country, 'Tis of Thee

Melody
Vs 1- Violin
Vs 2- Violin and Vocal sing vs 1
Vs 3- Cello then Viola/piano/harp
Vs 4- Guitar then Banjo
Vs 5- majority and Vocal sing vs 2 or 3

Guitar

Unknown
Tracey C. McKibben with addtional parts by N. Munger

Regal ♩= 98

Maestoso

©2023 for N. Munger parts

YANKEE DOODLE

Yankee Doodle is a well-known rollicking tune that has caused more quarrels among historians and musicians than any other American song. No one knows which of the five countries, that claims the tune as "theirs," the tune comes from!

The tune came to America in 1775 when the British were involved in the French and Indian War and saw the American soldiers. The smartly dressed British officers and men were poking fun at the US troops when Dr. Richard Shuckburg created the famous lyrics.

Yankee is thought to come from the Native Americans pronouncing the word "English", while the word "doodle" comes from an English term meaning "do-little" or "silly". "Macaroni" is not the pasta you're thinking it is. This word was used in England at the time to refer to a very well dressed, stylish, and worldly man. The point being that you couldn't just stick a feather in your hat and instantly be upper class.

Unfortunately for the British, their joke went sour against them. The Yankees loved the tune and words and turned it into a life-long troop rallying tune for multiple wars, patriotic events, and general American fun.

<u>Yankee Doodle</u>
Yankee Doodle went to town
Riding on a pony;
Stuck a feather in his cap
And called it macaroni.

Yankee Doodle keep it up,
Yankee Doodle dandy,
Mind the music and the step,
And with the girls be handy.

SCAN HERE FOR PRACTICE RECORDINGS

PRACTICE NOTES

Yankee Doodle

Guitar

Vs 1: Violin Melody, Piano/Harp Melody
Vs 2: Guitars Melody, Banjos Melody
Vs 3: Viola Melody, Cello Melody, Vocalists Melody
Vs 4: Drum Solo w/ chord backup guitar and banjo
Chorus: ALL and Vocal

Traditional
Nina Munger

(1)

9

(2) D D D A D G

18

A D

27

```
            0 2 0   0 2 3       0         0 2 0   0 2 3 0         0
              2           2 0     2         2           2   3 2     3  3
                                4
```

(3)

37

46

(4) D D D A D G A

55

D G G D D G G D A D

64

©2023

Yankee Doodle

2

Chorus

73 *rit.*

f

AMERICA THE BEAUTIFUL

"America the Beautiful" was inspired by the view from the top of Pikes Peak in Colorado. In the summer of 1893, poet Katharine Lee Bates was teaching English at Colorado College in Colorado Springs, Colorado. Later she remembered:

One day some of the other teachers and I decided to go on a trip to 14,000-foot Pikes Peak. We hired a prairie wagon. Near the top we had to leave the wagon and go the rest of the way on mules. I was very tired. But when I saw the view, I felt great joy. All the wonder of America seemed displayed there, with the sea-like expanse.
-Katharine Lee Bates

On the pinnacle of the mountain a poem started to come to her. She wrote down the words after returning to her hotel room. The poem was first published with the name "Pikes Peak" in the Independence Day edition of the church periodical "The Congregationalist" in 1895. Over the years, several existing pieces of music were adapted to the poem. A hymn tune composed by church organist and choirmaster Samuel A. Ward in 1882 was first published with Bates' poem in 1910 as "America the Beautiful."

SCAN HERE FOR PRACTICE RECORDINGS

Practice Tip!

We are going to be performing this one with the whole audience singing along! To help practice this at home, see if your family can sing along while you play! Try not to let it throw you off.

AMERICA THE BEAUTIFUL

We will play together once, then the vocalists and the audience will join in! We most likely will only do one verse, but I wanted to include all of the verses here!

America The Beautiful
O beautiful for spacious skies, for amber waves of grain
For purple mountain majesties, above the fruited plain
America, America, God shed His grace on thee
And crown thy good with brotherhood, from sea to shining sea

O beautiful for Pilgrim feet, whose stern impassioned stress
A thoroughfare for freedom beat, across the wilderness
America, America, God mend thine every flaw
Confirm thy soul in self control, Thy liberty in law

O beautiful for heroes proved, in liberating strife
Who more than self their country loved, and mercy more than life
America, America, May God thy gold refine
Till all success be nobleness, and every gain divine

O beautiful for patriot dream, that sees beyond the years
Thine alabaster cities gleam, undimmed by human tears
America, America, God shed His grace on thee
And crown thy good with brotherhood, from sea to shining sea

America The Beautiful

Samuel A. Ward
S. Murdock

PRACTICE NOTES

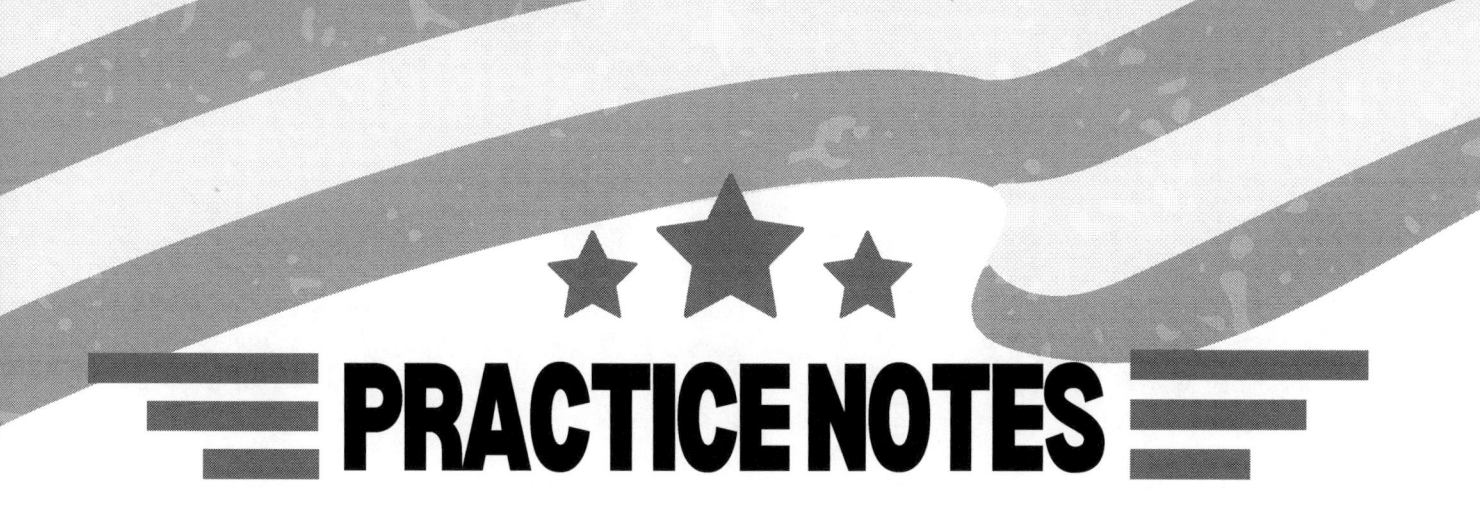

ASHOKAN FAREWELL

" 'Ashokan Farewell' was named for Ashokan, a camp in the Catskill Mountains not far from Woodstock, New York. It's the place where Molly Mason and I have run the Ashokan Fiddle & Dance Camps for adults and families since 1980.

I composed Ashokan Farewell in 1982 shortly after our camp had come to an end for the season. I was feeling a great sense of loss and longing for the music, the dancing and the community of people that had developed at Ashokan that summer. I was having trouble making the transition from a seclude woodland camp with a small group people..., back to life as usual...." – www.jayandmolly.com

Filmmaker Ken Burns heard the album Jay and Molly recorded the tune on and soon contacted them to use it in his upcoming PBS Series The Civil War. Jay and Molly (and their band) played for most of the music, as well as the now famous violin solo opening to the show.

Major Sullivan Ballou of the 2nd Rhode Island Volunteers was 32-years-old at the beginning of the Civil War. He was born in Smithfield, Rhode Island and after attending the National Law School in Ballston New York he was admitted to the Rhode Island Bar. Ballou married Sarah on October 15, 1855 and they had two sons, Edgar and William. Ballou was a Republican and strong supporter of President Lincoln. He volunteered the spring of 1861, and shortly died after penning his letter (made famous in the Civil War documentary) on July 21, 1861.

WE WILL PERFORM IT JUST LIKE THIS

SCAN HERE FOR PRACTICE RECORDINGS

PRACTICE NOTES

Ashokan Farewell

Jay Ungar
S. Murdock

©2023 Snake River Strings Co.

Ashokan Farewell

Ashokan Farewell

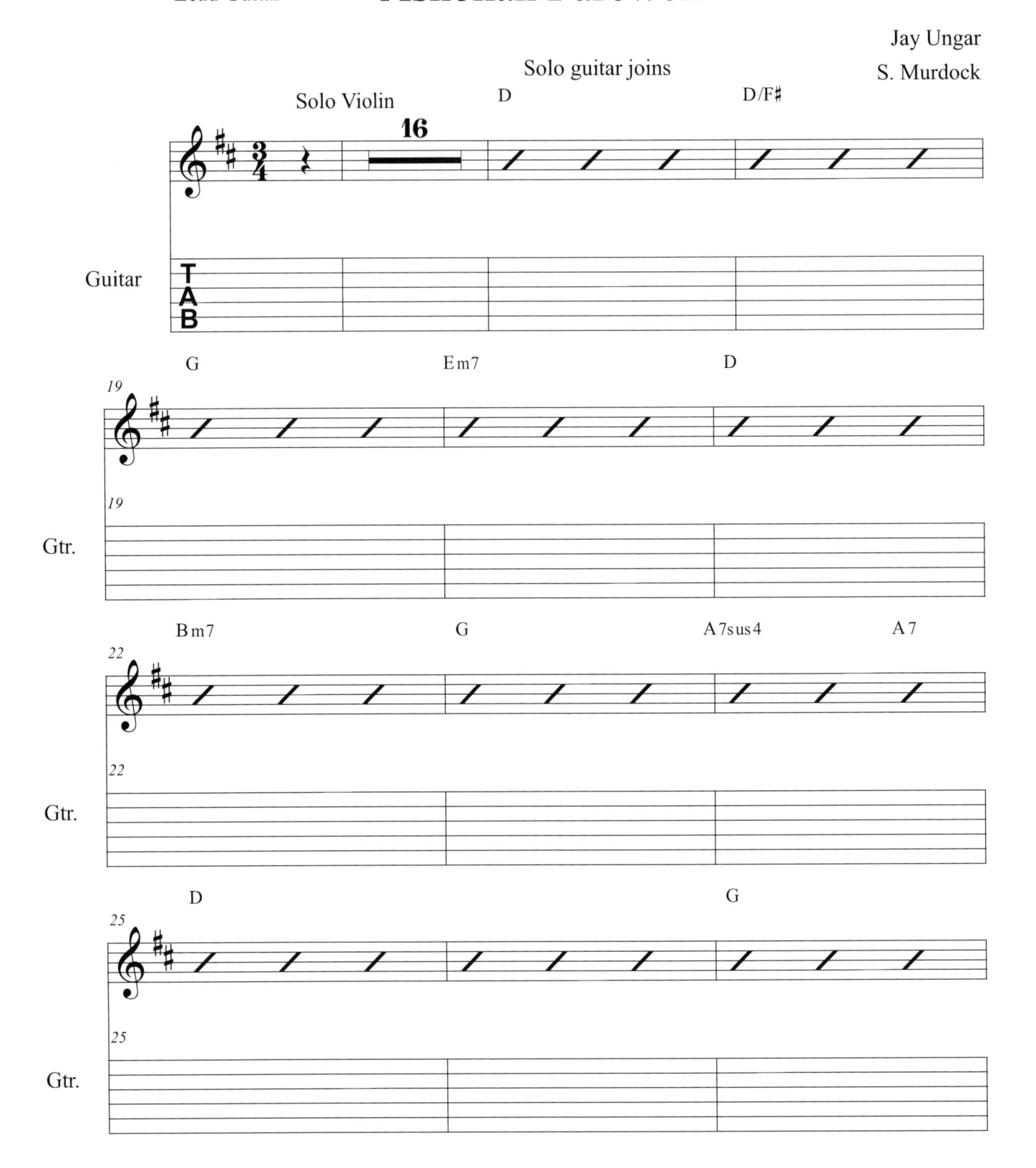

Lead Guitar

Jay Ungar
S. Murdock

Ashokan Farewell

Em7	D	D/F#
A7	D	
D/F#	G	D
	Bm	A
A/G	D/F#	C

Ashokan Farewell

Ashokan Farewell

SOLDIER'S JOY

Solomon Conn, a Civil War soldier with Company B of the 87th Indiana Volunteers, recorded a list of his travels and battles on the back of his violin, turning the instrument into a unique document of his adventures and military record. This violin is now on display at the National Museum of American History in Washington D.C.

Conn's fiddle may be very different from the elegance of the Stradivari instruments in the museum's collection, but the fact that Solomon carried it with him throughout his Civil War travels and used it as a travel diary proves that it must have been important to him and to other soldiers in his regiment.

Music was an essential part of life during the Civil War for soldiers and civilians on both sides of the war. More than just offering a break from the miseries of battle and camp life, music was part of larger political and military battles raging throughout the war.

It's fun to imagine what tunes were played on that fiddle each evening. One tune that was sure to have been played was Soldier's Joy. Soldier's Joy is one of, if not the most, popular fiddle tunes in history. The name of a Civil War drink (beer, whiskey, and morphine), and the name of a still popular fiddle/dance tune—both guaranteed to bring soldiers "joy"

SCAN HERE FOR PRACTICE RECORDINGS

PRACTICE NOTES

Soldier's Joy

Guitar

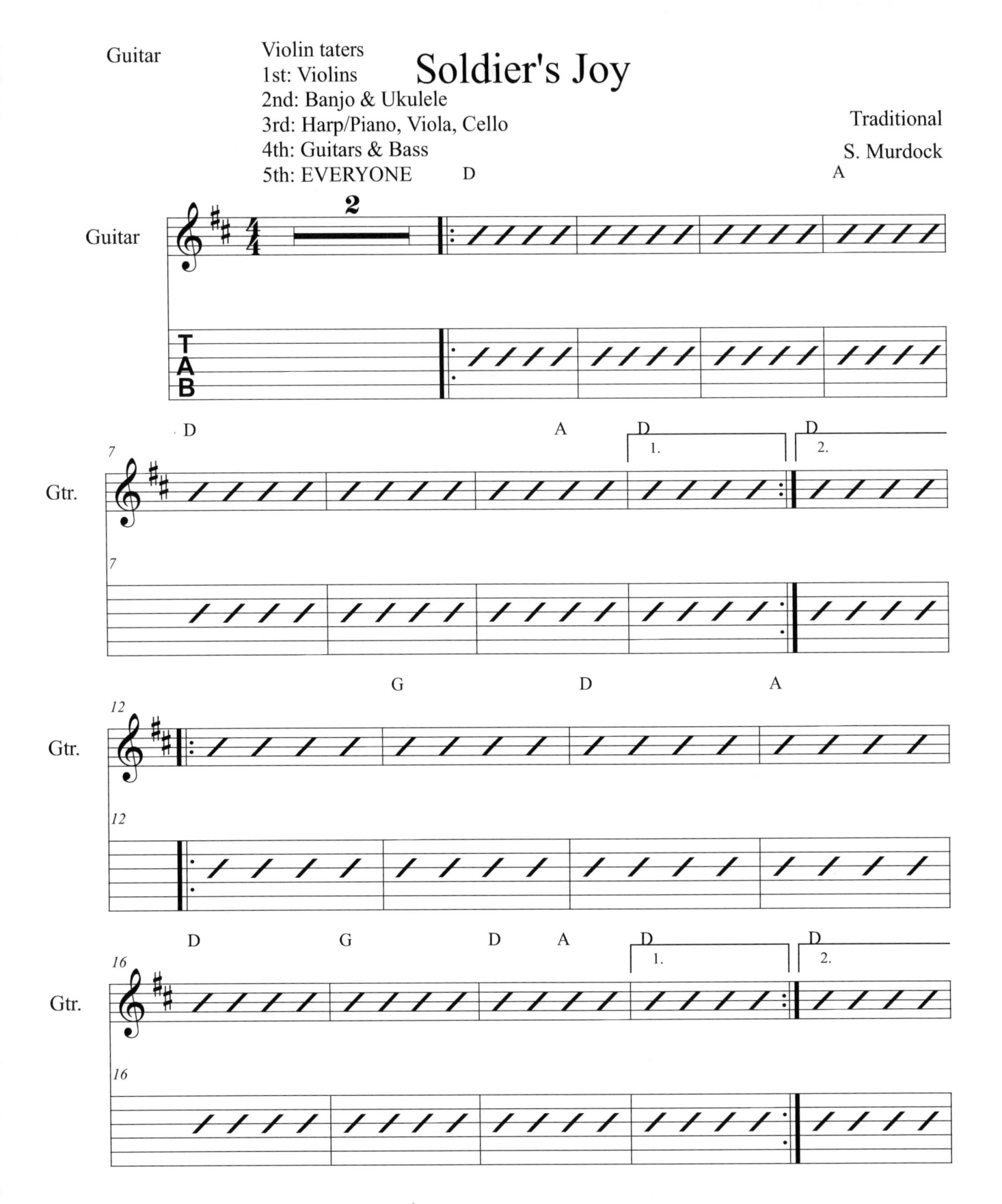

Violin taters
1st: Violins
2nd: Banjo & Ukulele
3rd: Harp/Piano, Viola, Cello
4th: Guitars & Bass
5th: EVERYONE

Traditional
S. Murdock

Repeat 3 more times from measure 3

©2023 SnakeRiverStringsCo

Soldier's Joy

Repeat one more time from the beginning of guitar solo

Adv Guitar

Violin taters
1st: Violins
2nd: Banjo & Ukulele
3rd: Harp/Piano, Viola, Cello
4th: Guitars & Bass
5th: EVERYONE

Soldier's Joy

Traditional
S. Murdock

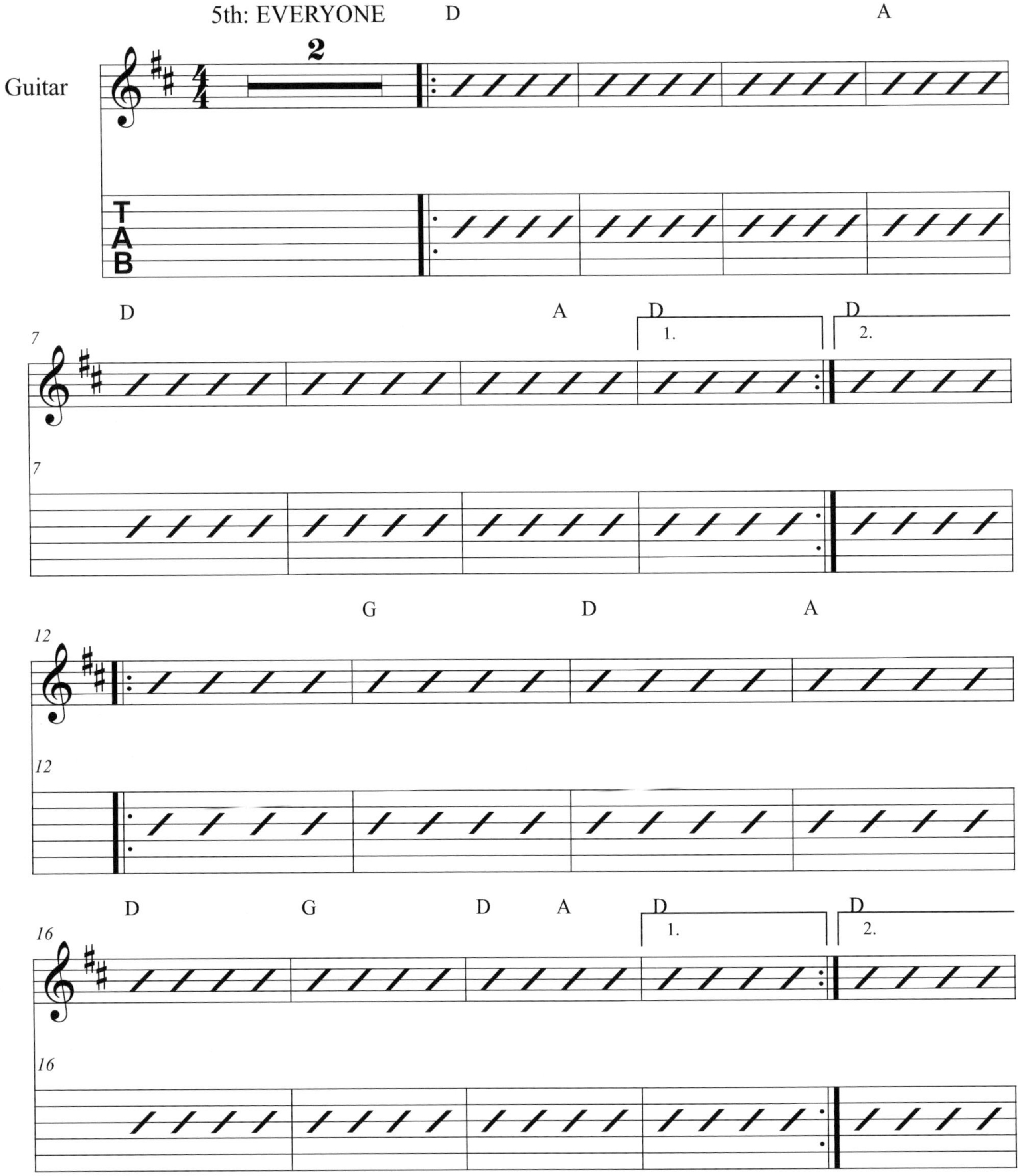

Repeat 3 more times from measure 3

Soldier's Joy

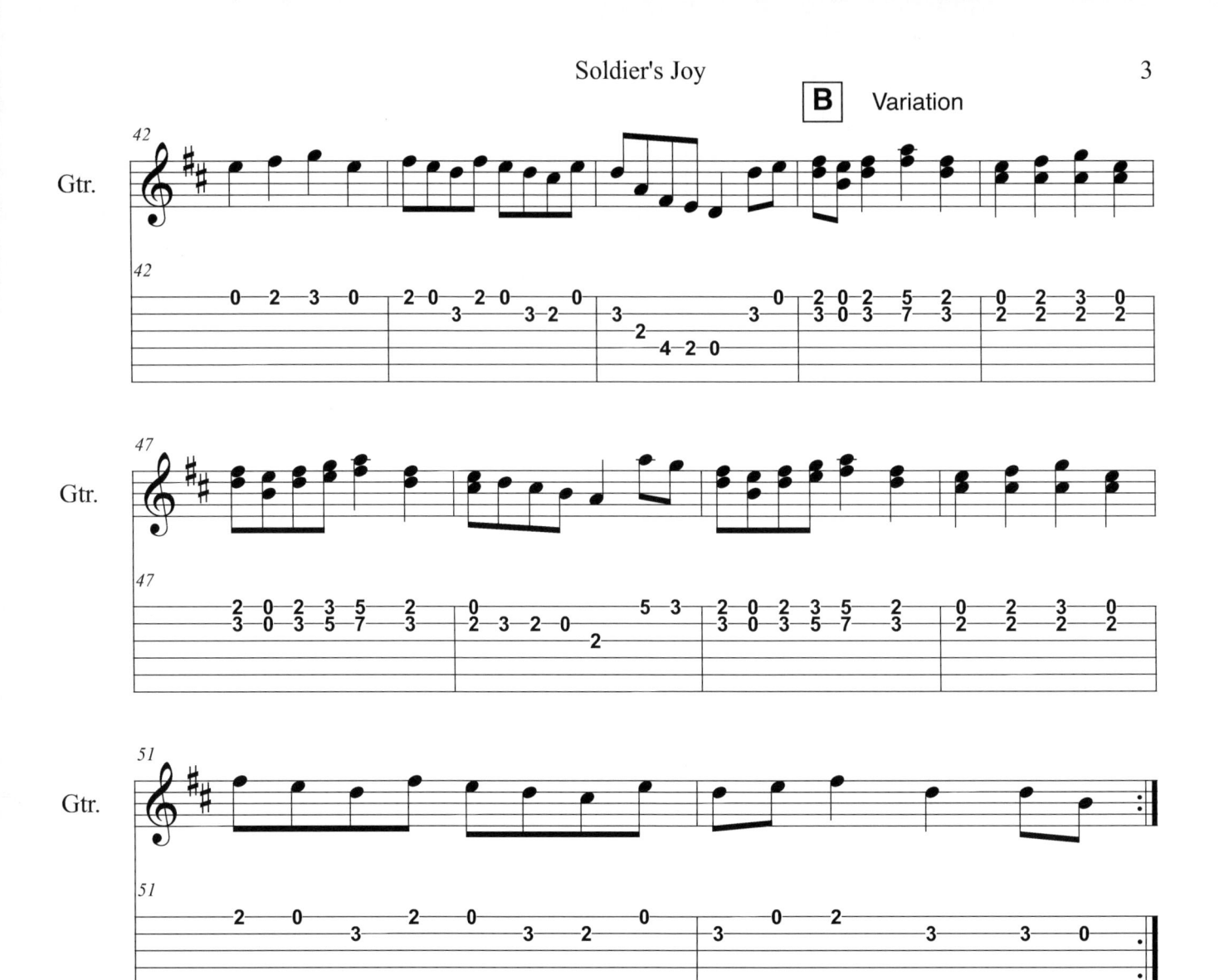

Soldier's Joy

THIS LAND IS YOUR LAND

The Great Depression was dragging into its 10th year and Woody Guthrie was sick of hearing "God Bless America" for the umpteenth time. It was driving him nutty! He felt it was too sappy, too blindly patriotic, and too far fetched from what Americans including himself were feeling at the time. He knew first hand how tough life could be for poor folk. He had hopped trains and hitchhiked back and forth across the country since a teenager. He chronicled the stories of sorrows, hopes, dreams, and adventures from the people he met in song.

In February 1940, Guthrie decided to fight music with music. In his reaction to God Bless America, he worked up a simple song that tried to capture his love for the American landscape, while also trying to point out that a lot of Americans weren't feeling blessed at all.

SCAN HERE FOR PRACTICE RECORDINGS

This Land is Your Land

This land is your land, this land is my land
From California to the New York Island;
From the red wood forest to the Gulf Stream waters
This land was made for you and me.

As I was walking that ribbon of highway,
I saw above me that endless skyway:
I saw below me that golden valley:
This land was made for you and me.

I've roamed and rambled and I followed my footsteps
To the sparkling sands of her diamond deserts;
And all around me a voice was sounding:
This land was made for you and me.

When the sun came shining, and I was strolling,
And the wheat fields waving and the dust clouds rolling,
As the fog was lifting a voice was Chanting:
This land was made for you and me.

THIS LAND IS YOUR LAND

★ **guitar intro: DD DD GG GG**

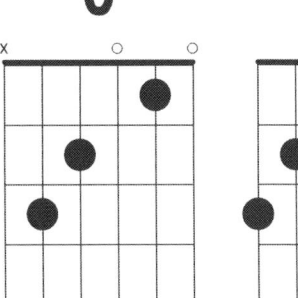

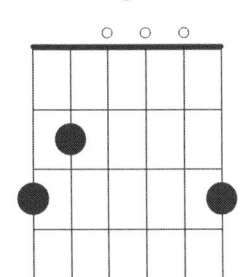

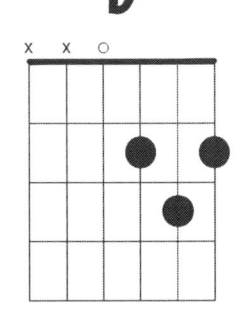

         C   G
This land is your land, this land is my land
         D   G
From California to the New York Island;
                     C   G
From the red wood forest to the Gulf Stream waters
D   G
This land was made for you and me.

*Banjo solo (play chords through verse)

As I was walking that ribbon of highway,
I saw above me that endless skyway:
I saw below me that golden valley:
This land was made for you and me.

*Fiddle solo

I've roamed and rambled and I followed my footsteps
To the sparkling sands of her diamond deserts;
And all around me a voice was sounding:
This land was made for you and me.

*Guitar solo

THIS LAND IS YOUR LAND

When the sun came shining, and I was strolling,
And the wheat fields waving and the dust clouds rolling,
As the fog was lifting a voice was Chanting:
This land was made for you and me.

*Solo

This land is your land, this land is my land
From California to the New York Island;
From the red wood forest to the Gulf Stream waters
This land was made for you and me.

⭐ **TAG Ending: DD DD GG GG**

This Land is Your Land - Solo

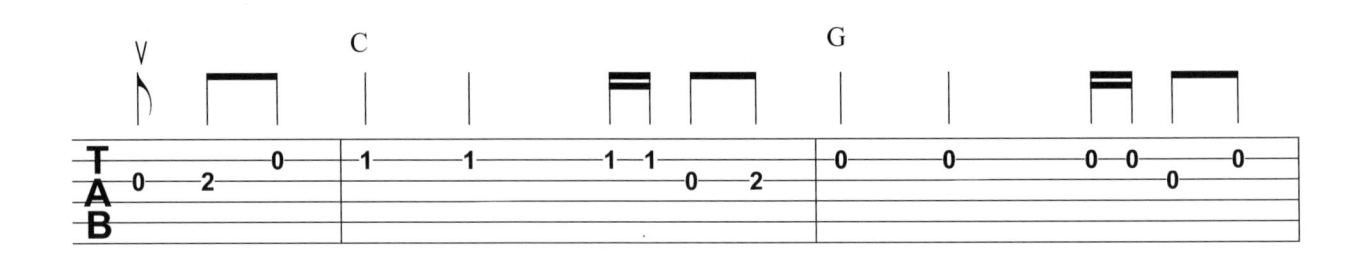

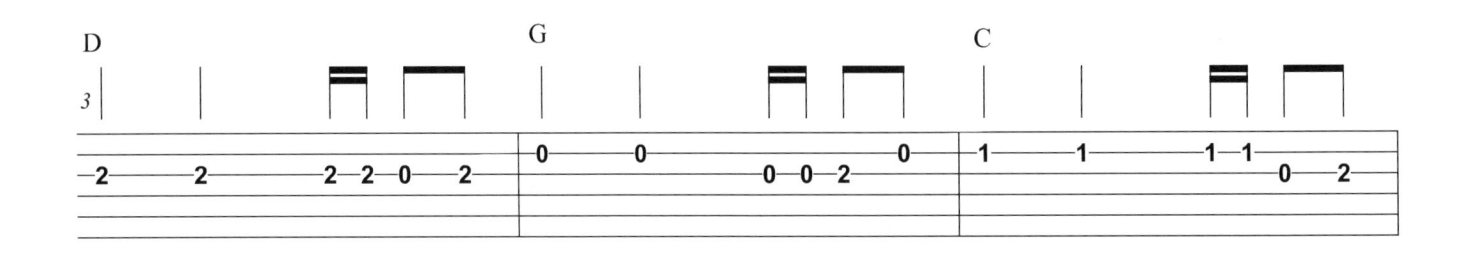

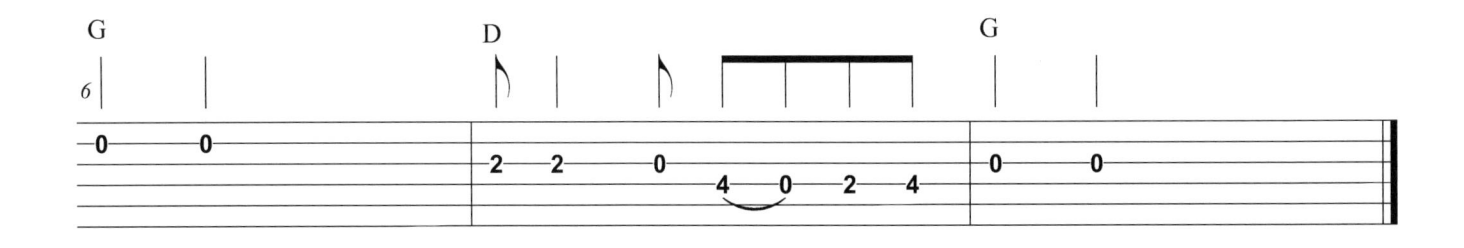

PRACTICE NOTES

STAR SPANGLED BANNER

Francis Scott Key was an American lawyer and poet. He and many other Americans were not at all happy when the U.S. declared war on Great Britain, starting the War of 1812. America was greatly out numbered in fleet and men compared to British. In August 1814, British forces raided the White House and many other government buildings. The destruction was a huge blow to our country, but it moved a lot of Americans, including F.S. Key to get involved in the war effort.

On September 13, 1814, Key and a U.S. officer rowed over to a British warship at the mouth of the Patapsco River outside of Baltimore, Maryland. Their mission was to seek the release of some prisoners.

While the meeting and dinner went well, Key and his companions were held on board the British ship. They had seen too much of the British's plan of attack. While meeting with Key, the British had set up to blast Fort McHenry, about eight miles away, into submission. Once taken over, the British could raid the city, like Washington.

Key and his companions heard the more than 1,500 rockets and shells fired at their fort and wondered if they would ever see their homeland as America again.

As dawn neared, Key squinted through the gloom and smoke. He prepared himself to see the British flag flying over Fort McHenry. But wait! Was it? It couldn't be? It WAS! A huge American flag still proudly waved out to prove the attack had failed.

As soon as he was released, Key pulled an envelope from his pocket and began writing the words to our National Anthem. He then chose a well know tune to put it to.

It became a hit immediately! A music printer took the liberty to change the title from Defense of Fort McHenry, to The Star-Spangled Banner. It became the National Anthem in 1931 when the bill passed Congress and was signed into law by President Herbert Hoover.

STAR SPANGLED BANNER

O say can you see by the dawn's early light,
What so proudly we hailed at the twilight's last gleaming,
Whose broad stripes and bright stars through the perilous fight,
O'er the ramparts we watched, were so gallantly streaming?
And the rocket's red glare, the bombs bursting in air,
Gave proof through the night that our flag was still there;
O say does that star-spangled banner yet wave,
O'er the land of the free and the home of the brave.

SCAN HERE FOR PRACTICE RECORDINGS

A recent poll reports that two thirds of Americans do not know all the words to the first verse of our own National Anthem. Why don't you challenge yourself to memorize it by the concert!

THIS IS WHERE WE GOT INSPIRATION

The Star-Spangled Banner

Guitar

John Stafford Smith

This version will be played at the very beginning of the concert with just three guitar players when the colors are posted, so this will be auditioned! We will play the other version with everyone later in the concert.

The Star- Spangled Banner
National Anthem of America

Guitar

Francis Scott Key, John Stafford Smith
Based off of Master Gunnery Sergeant Peter Wilson's arrangement
Nina Munger

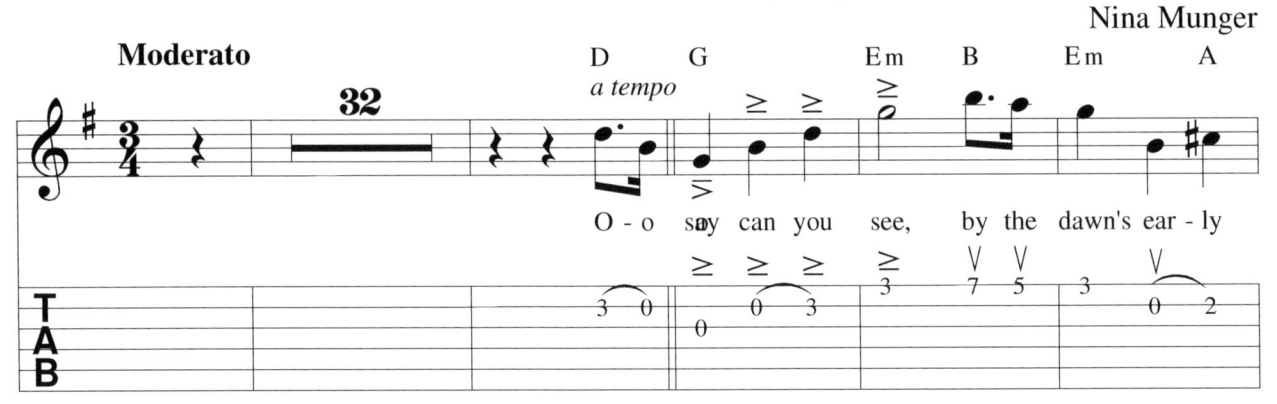

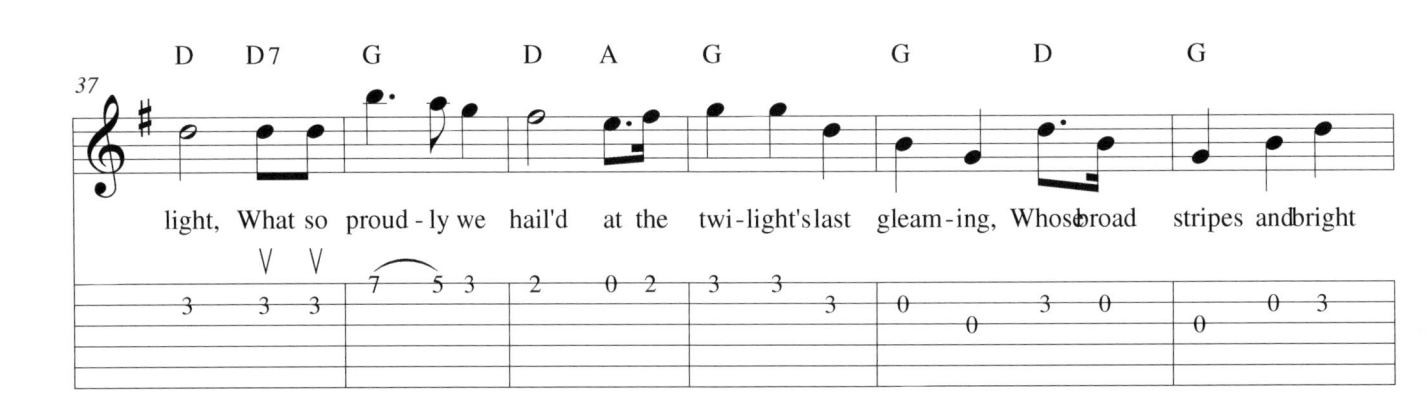

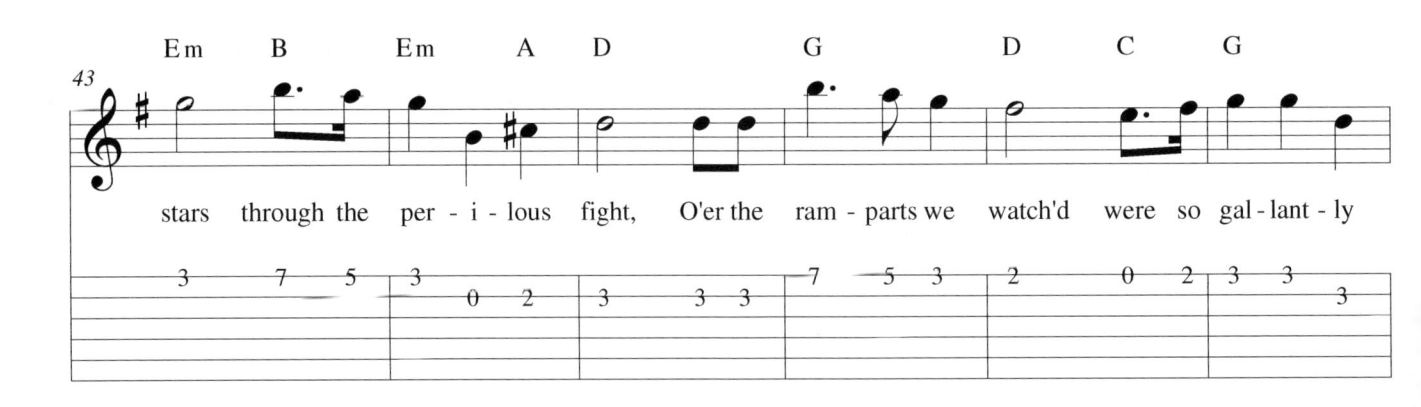

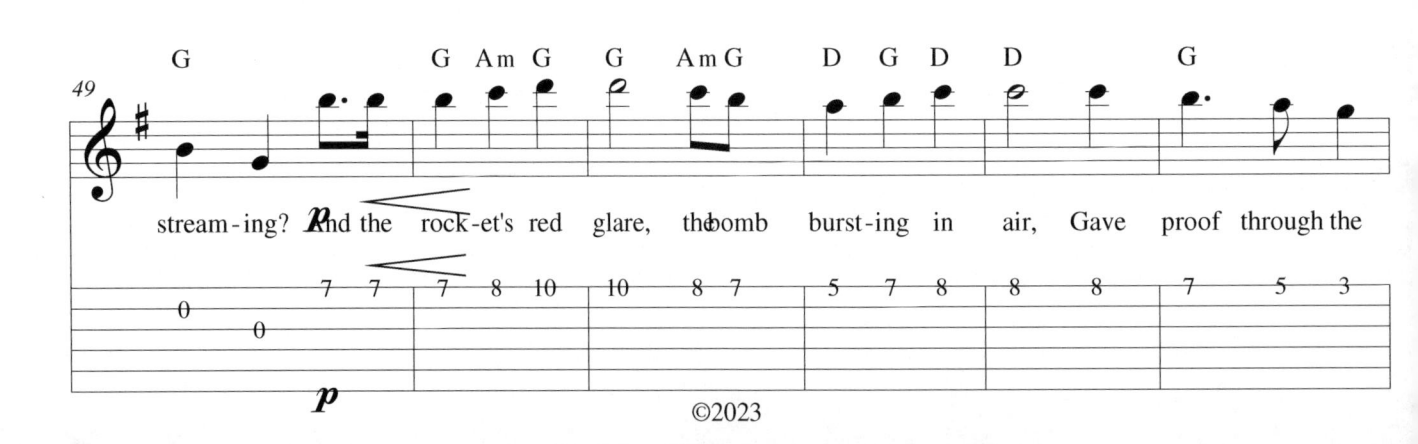

©2023

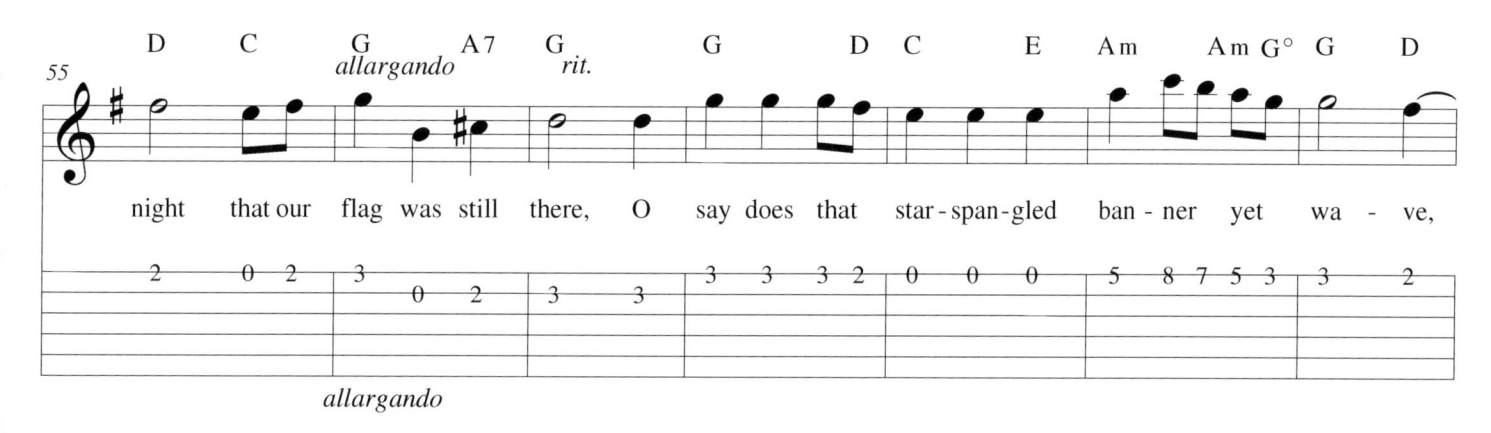

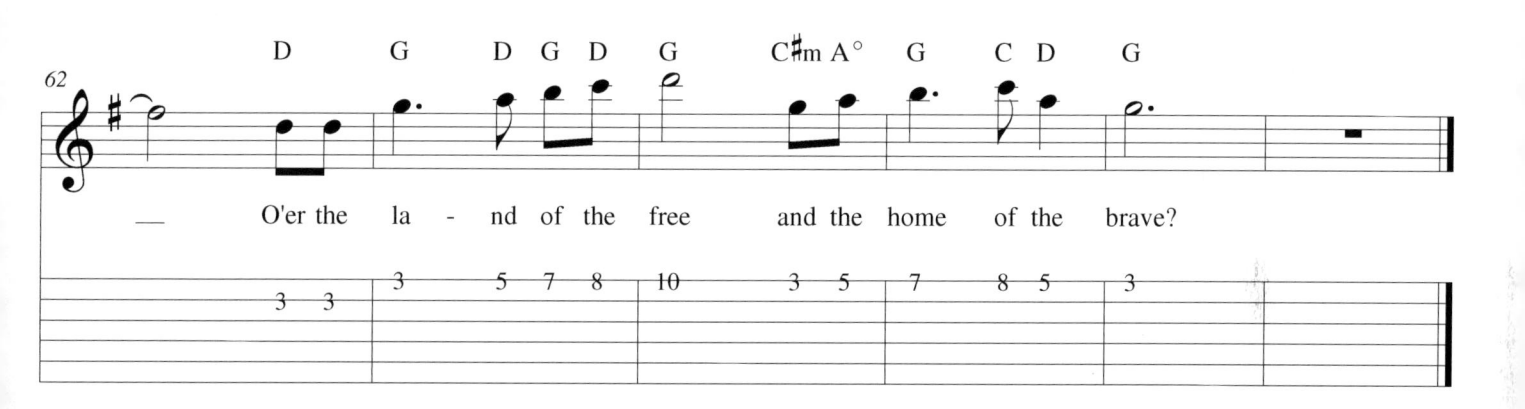

The Star-Spangled Banner

night that our flag was still there, O say does that star-spangled ban-ner yet wa - ve,

O'er the la - nd of the free and the home of the brave?

PRACTICE NOTES

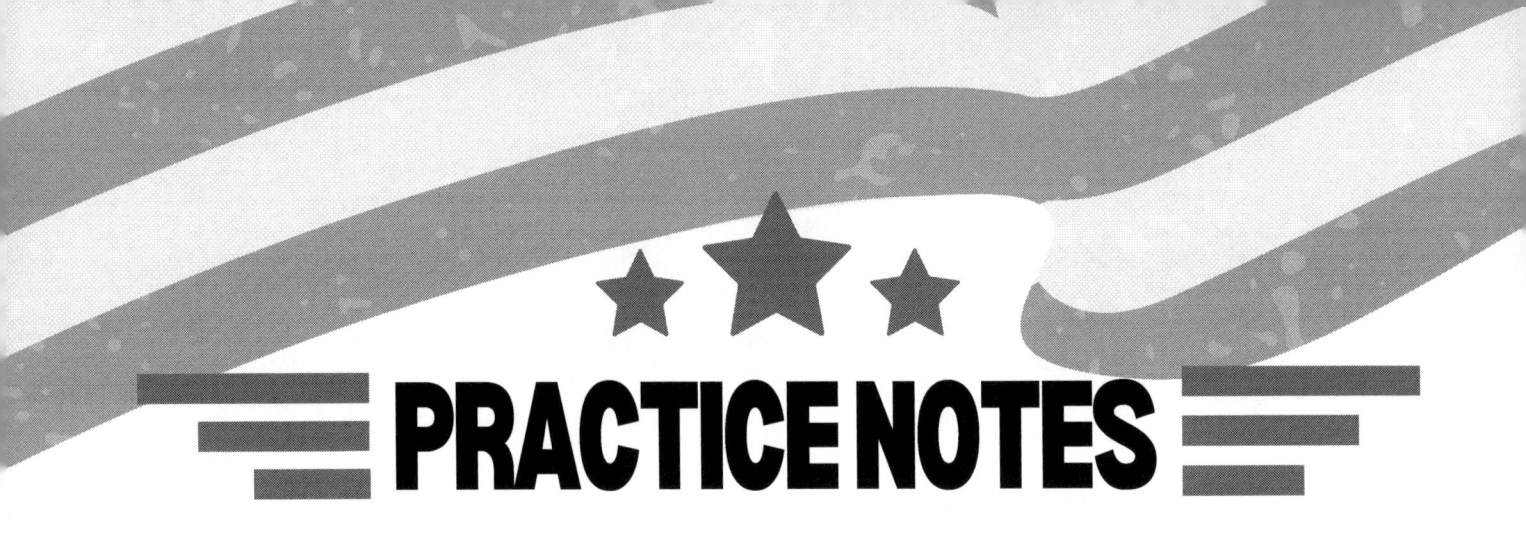

ARMED FORCES MEDLEY

The Armed Forces Medley, sometimes known as the Armed Forces Salute, is the collection of the official songs of the six military uniformed services of the United States (however we will not be playing the theme song of the Space Force). We will be playing them in the following order...

1. Army
2. Marines
3. Coast Guard
4. Air Force
5. Navy

Members of each military branch stand as their branches' anthem is played. When serving, all soldiers are expected to memorize these anthems, and they stand and sing them from heart.

This piece focuses heavily on the percussion section, so make sure to practice along with the percussion practice track (no matter your instrument)!

SCAN HERE FOR PRACTICE RECORDINGS

QUIZ!

1. What does Semper Paratus mean?
2. What are the key signatures for each song?
3. Which anthem is the oldest?
4. What year was this first performed?
5. Which one is your favorite?

1. Always Ready 2. C C G G D 3. Marines Hymn 4. 1990 5. Varies

PRACTICE NOTES

ARMED FORCES MEDLEY

⭐ ARMY: THE CAISSONS GO ROLLING ALONG

C
First to fight for the right,

And to build the Nation's might,
      G   C
And the Army goes rolling along.

Proud of all we have done,

Fighting till the battle's won,
      G   C
And the Army goes rolling along.

      G7   C
Then it's hi! hi! Hey!
    F   C
The Army's on its way.
Am   D7   G G7
Count off the cadence loud and strong;
        C   Em
For where'er we go,
F   C
we will always know
      G   G7   C
That the Army goes rolling along.

*Repeat all, then wait for the drum interlude

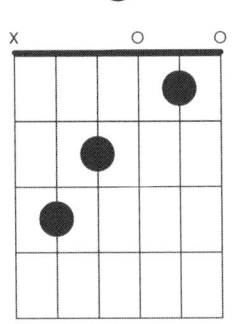

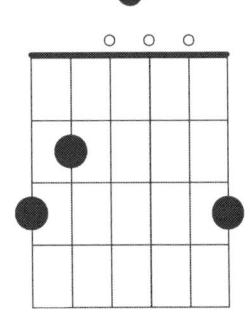

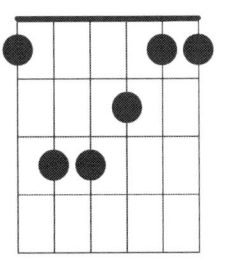

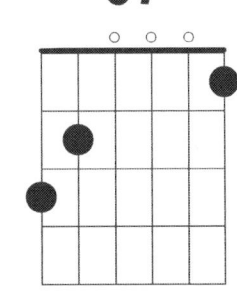

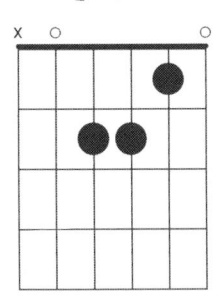

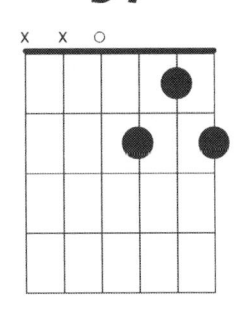

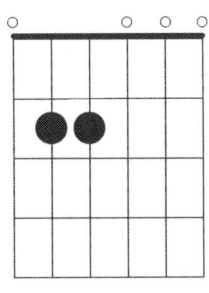

⭐ THE MARINES' HYMN

        C   G   C
From the halls of Montezuma
      G   G7   C
to the shores of Tripoli
     C   G   C
We fight our country's battles
     G   G7   C
In the air, on land, and sea.

        F   C
First to fight for the right and freedom,
       F   C   G
And to keep our honor clean,
     C   G   C
We are proud to claim the title
     G   G7   C
Of United States Marines!

Repeat all, then wait for the drum interlude

⭐ COAST GUARD: SEMPER PARATUS

G
We're always ready for the call,
   C   G
We place our trust in thee.
      D   G B7   Em
Through surf and storm and howling gale
     D   A7   D D7
High shall our purpose be.
G
Semper paratus is our guide,
    C   G
Our fame, our glory too.
     D   G   B7 Em Am
To fight to save or fight and die, Aye
G   A7 D G
Coast Guard we are for you.

Repeat all, then wait for the drum interlude

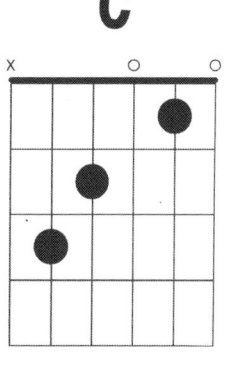

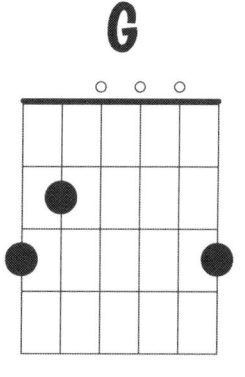

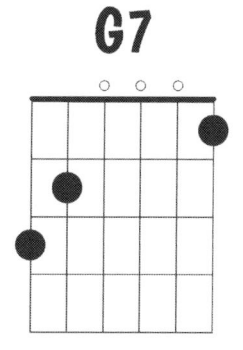

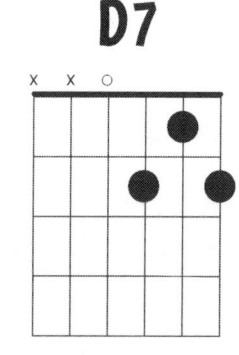

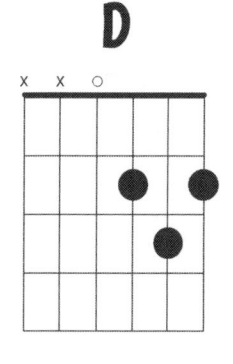

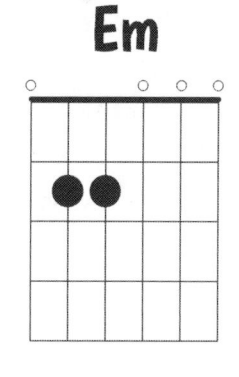

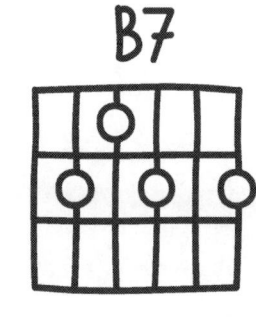

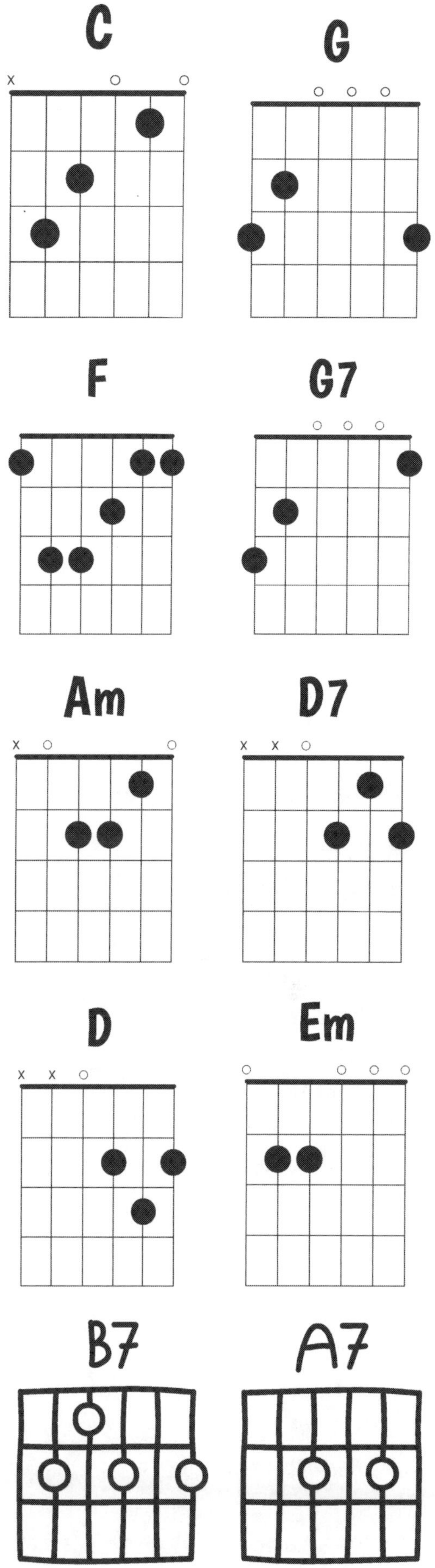

⭐ U. S. AIR FORCE

```
    G      D        G    Am A#dim G/B
Off we go, into the wide blue yonder,
    C       G         D
Climbing high into the sun.
    G      D        G    Am A#dim G/B
Here we come, zooming to meet our thunder,
    D      A         D D7
At 'em boys give 'er the gun.
    G      D        G    Am  A#dim G/B
Down we dive, spouting our flame from under,
    C            B7
Off with one hell uv a roar,
      Em   E7/D     Am/C   C#dim7
We live in fame or go down in flame,
         G            A  D7  G
Hey nothing will stop the U. S. Air Force.
```

A#dim

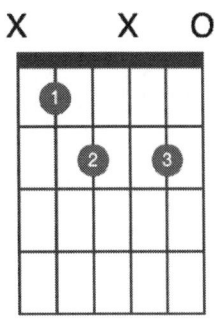

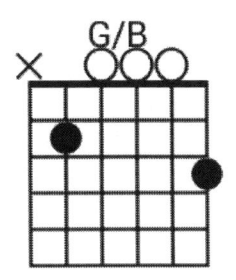

G/B

Repeat all, then wait for the drum interlude

⭐ U.S. NAVY: ANCHORS AWEIGH

```
    D       Bm
Anchors aweigh, my boys.
    D    A     D
Anchors aweigh.
    G        D
Farewell to college joys,
         E          A    A7
we sail at break of day ay ay ay
    D          Bm
Through our last night on shore,
    D    A     D
Drink to the foam.
    G        D
Until we meet once more,
           A       A7        D
Here's wishing you a happy voyage home.
```

Bm

Repeat all, then end :)

Armed Forces Medley- Guitar

Traditional
S. Murdock

♩ = 120

Army: The Cassions Go Rolling Along

A

fight for the right and to build the nations might, And the Army goes rolling a-
All we have done fighting til the battles won,

long. Proud of long. Then it's hi! Hi! Hey! the Army's on it's way;

Count off the cadence high and strong! for where 'er we go, we will always know that the

©Snake River Strings Co. 2023

Armed Forces Medley - Guitar

2

army goes rolling along First to

Marine Corps: The Marines' Hymn

From the halls of Montezuma to the shores of Tripoli, We
fight our country's battle's in the air on land and

Sea. First to fight for right and freedom, and to keep our honor

clean, We are proud to claim the title of U-

Armed Forces Medley - Guitar

ni - ted State Ma - rine! From the rine!

Coast Guard: Semper Paratus

We're al - ways rea - dy for the call, we place our trust in thee. Through surf and storm and howl - ing gale, high shall our pur - pose be. Sem - per par - a - tus is our guide, our fame our glo - ry too. To fight to save or fight and die, Aye Coast Guard we are for

Armed Forces Medley - Guitar

Air Force: U.S. Air Force Anthem

Off we go into the wide blue yonder, Climbing high into the sun. here we come, zooming to meet our thunder, at 'em boys give 'er the gun. down we dive, spouting our flame from under, Off with one hell-uv-a roar, we live in

E7/D Am/C C♯dim7 G A D G
fame or go down in flame, Hey no-thing will stop the U. S. Air Force
1. 2.
E
Navy: Anchors Aweigh
D Bm D A D
An - chors A - weigh, my boys, An - chors a - way.
G D E A A7 D
Fare - well to col - lege joys, we sail at break of day - ay - ay - ay. Through our last
Bm D A D G D
night on shore, drink to the foam. Un - til we meet once more, here's

6 Armed Forces Medley- Guitar

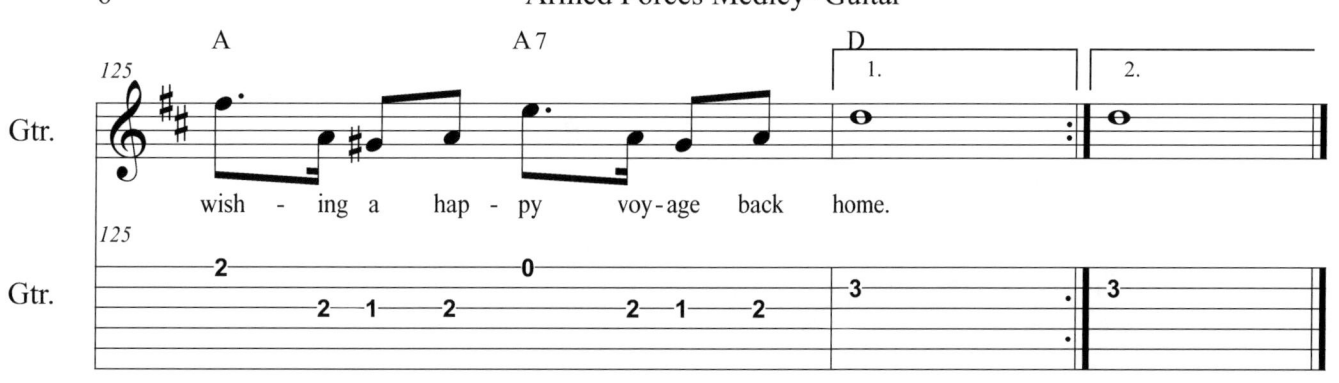

wish - ing a hap - py voy-age back home.

BUGLE CALL "TAPS"

""This song will by played by the cellos only! and it will be towards the end of the program when we retire the colors.

"Taps" is a bugle call sounded to signal "lights out" at the end of a military day, and during patriotic memorial ceremonies and military funerals conducted by the United States Armed Forces.

The tune is a variation of an earlier bugle call known as the "Scott Tattoo", which was used in the U.S. from 1835 until 1860. It was arranged in its present form by the Union Army Brigadier General Daniel Butterfield, a Medal of Honor recipient. Butterfield commanded the 3d Brigade, 1st Division, V Army Corps, Army of the Potomac while at Harrison's Landing, Virginia in July 1862, and wrote it to replace the customary firing of three rifle volleys at the end of burials during battle. Butterfield's version in July 1862 replaced a previous French bugle call used to signal "lights out". Butterfield's bugler, Oliver Wilcox Norton, of East Springfield, Pennsylvania, was the first to sound the new call. Within months "Taps" was used by both Union and Confederate forces. It was officially recognized by the United States Army in 1874.

SCAN HERE FOR PRACTICE RECORDINGS

PRACTICE NOTES

BORN IN THE USA

"Born in the U.S.A." is a song written and performed by Bruce Springsteen, and released in 1984 on the album of the same name. One of Springsteen's best-known singles, it was ranked 275th on Rolling Stone's list of "The 500 Greatest Songs of All Time." The song addresses the economic hardships of Vietnam veterans upon their return home, juxtaposed ironically against patriotic glorification of the nation's fighting forces.

This song will be performed by the rock group, mostly guitars, bass, drums, and voice students. However other instrumental students are invited to join in and come up with their own parts!

SCAN HERE FOR PRACTICE RECORDINGS

PRACTICE NOTES

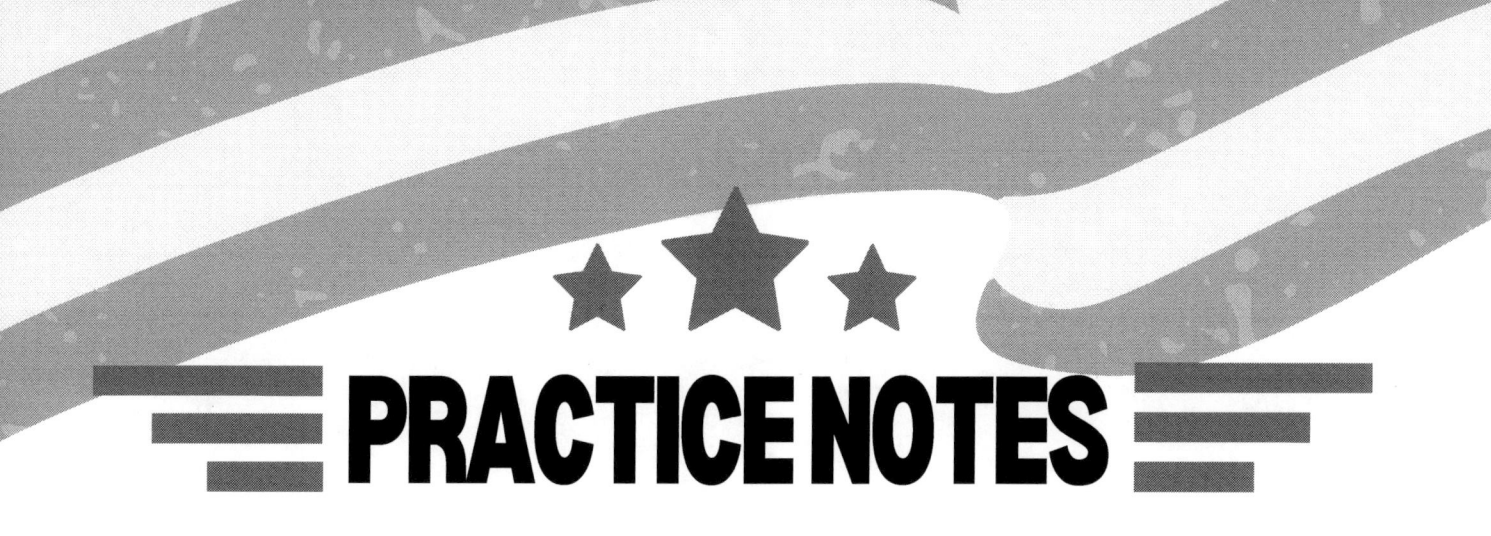

Born in the USA

Bruce Spingsteen

Got in a little hometown jam
So they put a rifle in my hand
Sent me off to a foreign land
To go and kill the yellow man

Born in the U.S.A.
I was born in the U.S.A.
I was born in the U.S.A.
I was born in the U.S.A.
Born in the U.S.A.

Come back home to the refinery
Hiring man says "Son if it was up to me"
Went down to see my V.A. man
He said "Son, don't you understand"

I had a brother at Khe Sahn fighting off the Viet Cong
They're still there, he's all gone

He had a woman he loved in Saigon
I got a picture of him in her arms now

Down in the shadow of the penitentiary
Out by the gas fires of the refinery
I'm ten years burning down the road
Nowhere to run ain't got nowhere to go

Born in the U.S.A.
I was born in the U.S.A.
Born in the U.S.A.
I'm a long gone Daddy in the U.S.A.
Born in the U.S.A.
Born in the U.S.A.
Born in the U.S.A.
I'm a cool rocking Daddy in the U.S.A.

GET TO KNOW YOU BINGO

Fill this sheet out by making new friends! Talk with your instructor at lessons or other students at studio class to find someone the square describes. All the squares must be someone different! Talk to your instructor or the front desk to receive a prize when you get bingo.

Performed at the summer recital	Plays a left-handed instrument	Takes voice lessons	Loves rock music	Goes to the Pocatello Studio
Competed in a fiddle competition	Uses alto clef for their instrument	Someone who plays acoustic guitar	Plays in school band, orchestra, or choir	Can play 3+ instruments
Has the same teacher as you	Is part of a band	**FREE SPACE**	Has more than $30 PB	Someone who plays the violin
Has an electric instrument	Someone who plays drums	Needs rosin for their instrument	Someone who plays the bass	Someone has played their instrument in a parade
Can play the mandolin	Goes to the Blackfoot Studio	Loves country music	Has a different teacher than you	Has a pink instrument

MASTERY REPETITIONS

Color in a star for each CORRECT repetition to develop mastery on a skill by practicing it 50 times!

I SPY music

MUSICAL CROSSWORD

About This Activity
Let's Crossword! is ideal for the beginning and intermediate student, helping them to learn note names in fun way. Figure out what each note name is, and then write the alphabet letter in the blank below the note. Once you discover what the word is you can start solving the puzzle!

Treble Clef

Let's Crossword!

Across

Down

www.makingmusicfun.net

Copyright © 2012 www.makingmusicfun.net

OUR FIRST FLAG

Our country's first flag.

YANKEE DOODLE DANDY

Made in the USA
Columbia, SC
17 August 2023